Financial Statement and Budget Report
1996-97

Return to an Order of the House of Commons dated 28 November 1995: for

Copy of Financial Statement and Budget Report 1996–97
as laid before the House of Commons by the Chancellor
of the Exchequer when opening the Budget

MICHAEL JACK

Treasury Chambers, 28 November 1995

Ordered by the House of Commons to be printed 28 November 1995

LONDON : HMSO

£17-00 net

House of Commons No. 30

Contents

Main Budget measures

Spending

- Firm control of public expenditure. Previous plans for 1996–97 reduced by £3¼ billion.

- Key priorities protected. Extra resources for:

  – schools

  – the National Health Service

  – the police.

- Reductions in costs of bureaucracy.

- Further shift to a more modern way of financing and managing public service projects to deliver better quality public services more efficiently. Substantial increase in activity under Private Finance Initiative and expansion of challenge funding to lever in private money and foster partnerships with the local community.

Tax

Helping people to keep more of what they earn and save

- Basic rate of income tax reduced to 24p.

- 20p lower rate band increased by £700.

- Tax on savings income cut from 25p to 20p.

- Main personal allowance increased by £240.

- Basic rate limit increased by £1,200.

- Inheritance tax threshold increased to £200,000.

Helping ensure people's needs are met in old age

- Package of help for the elderly needing long-term care.

Encouraging enterprise and helping business

- Small companies' rate of corporation tax reduced to 24p.

- More help for businesses facing higher rates bills following last year's revaluation.

- Employers' national insurance contributions cut by £500 million from April 1997.

1 The Budget

1.01   This Budget continues the work of recent years to promote sustainable economic growth with low inflation. The economy is in the fourth year of recovery, inflation has remained low and the public sector borrowing requirement (PSBR) has fallen sharply since 1993–94. The Budget will ensure that the PSBR continues to decline. And it will help the economy work better by improving incentives for individuals, ensuring better value for money from public spending and delivering services more efficiently in partnership with the private sector.

The public finances

1.02   The United Kingdom will best be able to compete in the world economy if tax and public spending take a smaller share of national income than at present.

1.03   The Government plans to reduce public spending to below 40 per cent of national income, while providing extra resources for priority areas.

1.04   The Government's aim on taxation is to make reductions when it is prudent to do so in order to improve the performance of the economy by strengthening incentives for individuals and businesses.

1.05   These tax and spending policies should ensure that the PSBR returns towards balance over the medium term. Table 1.1 summarises the projections of the public sector's finances from 1995–96 to 2000–01. These are set out in more detail in Chapter 4.

Table 1.1   The public sector's finances[1]

	Per cent of GDP					
	1995–96	1996–97	1997–98	1998–99	1999–00	2000–01
Receipts[2]	38¾	38½	38¾	39¼	39¼	39½
Current expenditure[2, 3]	41½	40½	39½	38¾	38	37
Current balance[2]	**−2¾**	**−2**	**−1**	**¼**	**1¼**	**2½**
Net capital spending[2, 4, 5]	1¾	1¼	1¼	1	1	¾
Financial deficit[2]	4½	3¼	2	½	−½	−1¾
Privatisation proceeds and other financial transactions	¼	½	0	0	0	0
Public sector borrowing requirement – per cent	**4**	**3**	**2**	**¾**	**−¼**	**−1½**
– £ billion	**29**	**22½**	**15**	**5**	**−2**	**−14**

[1] *In this and other tables, constituent items may not sum to totals because of rounding.*
[2] *Figures on a national accounts basis. See Annex B to Chapter 4.*
[3] *Includes depreciation of fixed capital.*
[4] *Capital spending net of depreciation and less capital transfer receipts.*
[5] *Does not include capital expenditure under the Private Finance Initiative (see Table 6.5).*

1.06   The PSBR for 1995–96 is now forecast to be £29 billion, £7 billion lower than in 1994–95. The Government is delivering its public spending plans. However, tax receipts have been lower than expected, contributing to higher borrowing than previously forecast. Part of this is attributable to lower growth of money GDP in 1995–96, but the underlying trend in tax receipts has also been less buoyant than expected. These developments feed through into the receipts projections for the later years.

1.07   Chart 1.1 illustrates trends in general government expenditure, receipts and the PSBR. Even taking account of lower than expected receipts, the PSBR is projected to continue falling year by year. The main factor behind this fall is the decline in spending relative to GDP. GGE(X) is expected to fall from over 43 per cent of GDP in 1992–93 to less than 41 per cent in 1996–97, and to below 39 per cent by 1998–99.

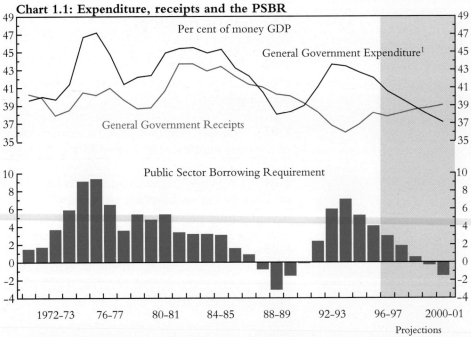

Chart 1.1: Expenditure, receipts and the PSBR

[1]GGE(X). *General government expenditure excluding privatisation proceeds and lottery financed spending, and net of interest and dividend receipts.*

1.08   The future improvement in the PSBR is driven by the Government's tax and spending policies, although above trend growth in GDP also makes a modest contribution. Firm control of the growth of spending within the Control Total plays the major part. Table 1.2 shows the cumulative effect on the PSBR compared with 1995–96 of keeping the growth in the Control Total well below the trend growth of GDP. It also shows the effects on the PSBR over time of the tax and national insurance measures in this Budget and the existing commitment to future real increases in road fuel and tobacco duties.

Table 1.2   The impact of tax and spending policies on the PSBR

	Per cent of GDP				
	1996–97	1997–98	1998–99	1999–00	2000–01
Change in PSBR compared with 1995–96 as a result of:					
Tax and NIC changes[1]	0·2	0·2	0·1	−0·1	−0·2
Effects of spending restraint[2]	−1·2	−1·8	−2·5	−3·0	−3·6
Total	**−0·9**	**−1·6**	**−2·4**	**−3·1**	**−3·8**

[1] *Changes from a 1995–96 indexed base. Includes continuing real annual increases in tobacco and fuel duties as previously announced. Reduction in receipts shown as positive, ie, increasing the PSBR.*
[2] *Spending restraint measured as the gap between the planned Control Total and what the Control Total would be if it were to grow in line with trend GDP after 1995–96.*

1.09   Table 1.3 shows the impact of the measures announced in this Budget on the public finances. The measures will be broadly neutral in their impact on the path for the PSBR over the next three years.

Table 1.3   Budget tax and spending measures

	£ billion		
	1996–97	1997–98	1998–99
Tax and NICs[1, 2]	−3·1	−4·6	−4·8
Public expenditure[3, 4]	−3·3	−3·7	−4·5
Total[5]	**−0·2**	**+0·9**	**+0·3**

[1] *Measured against an indexed base. Reduction in tax and NICs shown as negative. See Tables 1.5 and 5.1.*
[2] *Excludes impact of real increases in tobacco and fuel duties confirmed in this Budget but already taken into account in previous projections* +1·0 +1·1 +1·1
[3] *Changes in the Control Total since the 1994 Budget, and Budget measures affecting cyclical social security. See Table 6.2.*
[4] *In this and other tables, references to the 1994 Budget mean after allowing for the 8 December 1994 package of measures and after adjusting for classification changes.*
[5] *Increase in the PSBR shown as positive.*

The Budget measures

1.10   The main Budget measures are summarised on Page 4. Table 1.5 shows the revenue effects of the tax and NIC measures, and Table 1.6 sets out the new spending plans.

1.11   The measures:

- **keep the PSBR on a downward track**;

- **reduce public spending as a percentage of national income while protecting priority services, developing new partnerships with the private sector, and improving the efficiency of the public sector:**

  - there will be a further increase in the resources available to the national health service, schools and the police;

  - greater use of the Private Finance Initiative (PFI) will improve the efficiency and value for money of investment in public services; capital spending on private finance projects is expected to be about £2 billion in 1996–97 and to increase thereafter. More use of challenge funding will bring in extra resources to complement public funding while ensuring that spending is well targeted and meets real needs;

  - government departments' running costs are being reduced by 12 per cent in real terms over the next three years.

- **allow people to keep more of the money they earn and save; help ensure their needs will be met in old age; and encourage enterprise and business:**

  - the Government is approaching its target of a 20p basic rate of income tax in three ways: by cutting the basic rate from 25p to 24p; by increasing the 20p lower rate band by £700, and by cutting the tax on savings income from 25p to 20p. The main personal allowance will be increased by £240 and the basic rate limit by £1,200. The inheritance tax threshold will be increased to £200,000 so that people can pass on more of their wealth to their children;

  - to help elderly people who need long-term care, the Budget doubles to £16,000 the level of assets below which people can get some help from the Government for care in residential and nursing homes, and increases from £3,000 to £10,000 the level below which they need make no contribution out of their capital. The Budget also exempts from tax the benefits from a range of long-term care insurance policies. The Inland Revenue will consult on changes to pension rules allowing occupational pensioners the option of taking a variable pension, for example a larger one in later years when their needs are greatest in return for a smaller one earlier on. And there will be consultation on a range of proposals to encourage people to make provision for long-term care, studying particularly the experience of Partnership schemes in the United States;

– the small companies' rate of corporation tax will be reduced to 24p; the improvements in the transitional scheme for business rates will help business; and employers' national insurance contributions will be cut by £500 million from April 1997.

1.12   The growth in the PFI is illustrated by Chart 1.2. Departments expect to agree projects with a capital value of £14 billion by the end of 1998–99.

Chart 1.2: Cumulative level of capital spending expected to be agreed under the PFI, by Department

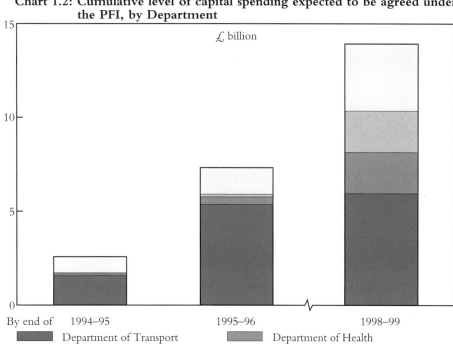

1.13   Partnerships between the public and private sectors extend beyond the PFI and challenge funding. For example, the growth in social housing provided by housing associations is financed partly by grants from the Housing Corporation which score as public expenditure and partly by private sector lending which does not. Nor does income earned by universities and further education colleges score in the public expenditure totals. In 1994–95, contributions levered in from the private sector totalling some £6¼ billion complemented government spending on public services and infrastructure.

1.14   There is also the effect of government subsidy through regional assistance and the Single Regeneration Budget. This is associated with considerable amounts of private investment in inner cities and regions of high unemployment. In total this investment amounted to £6½ billion in 1994–95. More details are given in Table 1.4.

Table 1.4   Private expenditure in partnership with the public sector: 1994–95

	£ billion
Private sector finance which complements public services	
Housing[1]	2¼
Higher/Further Education[2]	3
Other departmental schemes[3]	½
Overseas development co-funding[4]	½
Total	**6¼**
Private investment associated with public subsidy	
Regional assistance and cooperation with industry[5]	4
Urban regeneration[6]	2¼
Employment measures[7]	¼
Total	**6½**

[1] *Includes housing associations, local authority Housing Association Grant and Large Scale Voluntary Transfers.*
[2] *Recurrent income from non-government.*
[3] *Includes various measures covering heritage partnerships; food and agriculture; and aid joint-funding schemes.*
[4] *Private expenditure in joint-funding projects undertaken by the Commonwealth Development Corporation.*
[5] *Assistance to UK industry eg regional selective assistance; business start ups; research and development co-funding.*
[6] *Measures throughout UK such as urban development corporations, English Partnerships and City Challenge.*
[7] *Private sector contributions to training programmes.*

1.15   Table 1.7 summarises the Government's revenue and expenditure plans for 1995–96 and 1996–7. Charts 1.3 and 1.4 illustrate how the Government expects public expenditure to be allocated in 1996–97 and how this spending will be financed. Unlike Table 1.7, which breaks down expenditure by department, Chart 1.3 illustrates the pattern of expenditure by function. It relies on broad assumptions about the pattern of expenditure in Scotland, Wales and Northern Ireland and by local authorities so the figures can only be approximate. The charts do not show the considerable contribution to public services made by the private sector.

1.16   The Financial Statement and Budget Report contains the Government's assessment of the medium-term economic and budgetary position. It sets out the Government's tax and spending plans, including those for public investment, in the context of its overall approach to social, economic, and environmental objectives. After approval by Parliament for the purposes of Section 5 of the European Communities (Amendment) Act 1993, this report will form the basis of submissions to the European Commission under Articles 103(3) and 104c of the Treaty establishing the European Union.

Table 1.5   The Budget tax and national insurance measures[1]

	£ million yield (+)/cost (−) of measure			
	Changes from a non-indexed base	Changes from an indexed base		
	1996–97	1996–97	1997–98	1998–99
Income tax				
basic rate reduced to 24 per cent	−1 600	−1 600	−2 000	−2 100
personal allowances up by £100 over indexation	−1 190	−480	−700	−680
lower rate band widened by £500 over indexation	−520	−370	−530	−510
basic rate limit up by £200 over indexation	−270	−40	−80	−80
married couple's allowance – indexed	−90	0	0	0
Savings				
tax on savings income cut to 20p	−800	−800	−400	−450
Capital taxes				
inheritance tax threshold raised to £200,000	−155	−130	−250	−295
CGT retirement relief – age limit reduced	−10	−10	−40	−60
IHT business relief extended	★	★	★	−5
Other personal tax measures				
changes to employee share schemes	−15	−15	−10	−10
insurance benefits exempted from tax	−10	−10	−10	−10
vocational training relief extended	★	★	−5	−10
personal reliefs and tax credits extended to EEA nationals	−10	−10	−20	−20
Business taxation				
corporation tax – small companies' rate cut to 24 per cent	★	★	−95	−130
business rates transitional scheme amended	−135	−135	−95	−55
insurance equalisation reserves – tax relief	0	0	−100	−100
foreign income dividend scheme – changed	−10	−10	−10	−10
landfill tax introduced at £2/£7 per tonne	110	110	450	460
employer NICs main rate reduced by 0·2 per cent	0	0	−495	−580
VAT payments on account scheme – amended	600	600	0	0
Measures against avoidance and evasion	30	30	60	80
Excise duties				
petrol and diesel up by 3·5p a litre[2]	45	45	55	70
superunleaded petrol increased	25	25	25	25
fuel and gas oils up by 5 per cent in real terms	20	10	10	15
most tobacco duties up by 3 per cent in real terms[2]	25	25	25	30
beer, wine and most cider frozen	0	−150	−150	−155
spirits cut by 4 per cent	−30	−60	−60	−65
very strong cider up by 50 per cent	5	5	10	15
pools cut by 6 per cent and general betting by 1 per cent	−100	−100	−105	−105
car VED increased by £5, lorry VED frozen	115	−25	−25	−25
Other measures	−175	−45	−45	−30
Total[2]	**−4 145**	**−3 140**	**−4 590**	**−4 790**

[1] The measures and their revenue effects are set out in more detail in Chapter 5.   ★ = Negligible
[2] Costings exclude yield from previously announced excise duty increases confirmed in
this Budget: 1 910   1 015   1 070   1 120

Table 1.6   The new public spending plans[1]

	Changes from previous plans		New plans		
	1996–97	1997–98	1996–97	1997–98	1998–99
Control Total by department					
Social security[2]	1·0	0·5	76·8	79·6	82·2
Health[3]	0·5	0·1	33·8	34·2	35·0
DOE – Local government	0·4	0·5	31·3	31·4	31·5
DOE – Other	−0·8	−1·1	8·2	7·9	8·1
Scotland, Wales and N. Ireland[2]	0·0	0·1	29·4	29·7	29·9
Defence	−0·5	−0·4	21·4	21·9	22·6
Education and Employment	−0·4	0·1	14·0	14·5	14·5
Home Office	0·0	0·0	6·5	6·6	6·8
Transport	−0·2	−0·3	4·2	4·7	4·4
Other departments	−0·7	0·0	19·5	19·7	19·7
Local authority self-financed expenditure	0·6	0·7	12·5	13·0	13·3
Reserve	−3·2	−3·7	2·5	5·0	7·5
Control Total	**−3·2**	**−3·5**	**260·2**	**268·2**	**275·6**
Cyclical social security[4]	−0·1	−0·3	13·9	14·2	14·7
Central government debt interest[5]	0·6	2·1	22·3	24·0	24·0
Accounting adjustments	−0·8	−1·8	9·7	9·1	9·6
GGE(X)[6]	**−3·5**	**−3·5**	**306·1**	**315·5**	**324·0**
Real growth (per cent)					
Control Total			−1	½	½
GGE(X)			−½	½	½
GGE(X) as per cent of GDP			40½	39¾	38¾

£ billion

[1] *For definitions, rounding and other conventions, see notes in Annex A to Chapter 6.*
[2] *Excluding cyclical social security.*
[3] *Of which NHS*   0·1   0·1   33.1   33.9   34.7
[4] *Of which Budget policy changes*   −0·1   −0·2
[5] *Central government debt interest payments net of interest and dividend receipts from outside general government.*
[6] *General government expenditure excluding privatisation proceeds and lottery-financed spending and net of interest and dividend receipts.*

Table 1.7   The public finances in 1995–96 and 1996–97[1]

	£ billion				£ billion		
	1995–96		1996–97		1995–96		1996–97
	1994 Budget	Estimated outturn	Forecast		*1994 Budget*	Estimated outturn	New plans
RECEIPTS				**EXPENDITURE**			
Inland Revenue				**Control Total by department**			
Income tax	*70·1*	68·9	70·2	Social security	*72·6*	73·7	76·8
Corporation tax	*26·4*	24·7	26·6	Health	*32·9*	32·9	33·8
Petroleum revenue tax	*0·7*	0·9	1·0	DOE – Local government	*30·3*	30·3	31·3
Capital gains tax	*0·8*	0·9	1·0	DOE – Other	*9·0*	9·1	8·2
Inheritance tax	*1·5*	1·5	1·5	Scotland, Wales and N. Ireland	*28·9*	29·0	29·4
Stamp duties	*2·0*	2·0	2·4	Defence	*21·7*	21·2	21·4
				Education and employment	*14·2*	14·2	14·0
Customs and Excise				Home Office	*6·4*	6·6	6·5
Value added tax	*48·1*	44·0	47·9	Transport	*4·4*	4·6	4·2
Fuel duties	*16·0*	15·5	17·4	Other departments	*21·2*	21·5	19·5
Tobacco duties	*7·2*	7·2	7·7	Local authority self-financed			
Alcohol duties	*5·6*	5·6	5·7	expenditure	*11·7*	12·3	12·5
Betting and gaming duties	*1·2*	1·6	1·7	Reserve	*3·0*		2 5
Customs duties	*2·1*	2·3	2·4				
Agricultural levies	*0·2*	0·1	0·2	**Control Total**	**256·3**	**255·5**	**260·2**
Air passenger duty	*0·3*	0·3	0·3	Cyclical social security	*14·0*	14·0	13·9
Insurance premium tax	*0·7*	0·6	0·7	Central government debt interest[5]	*20·5*	20·5	22·3
Landfill tax			0·1	Accounting adjustments	*8·8*	9·6	9·7
Other				**GGE(X)[6]**	**299·7**	**299·6**	**306·1**
Vehicle excise duties	*4·0*	4·1	4·3	Privatisation proceeds	*–3·0*	–3·0	–4·0
Oil royalties	*0·5*	0·6	0·5	Other adjustments[7]	*5·1*	5·5	6·2
Business rates[2]	*13·8*	13·6	14·7				
Other taxes and royalties[3]	*15·0*	15·3	15·5				
Social security contributions	*44·6*	44·4	46·9				
Total taxes and social security contributions	**260·9**	**254·2**	**268·7**				
Other receipts[4]	*17·9*	17·7	16·1				
General government receipts	**278·7**	**271·9**	**284·8**	**General government expenditure**	*301·8*	**302·1**	**308·3**

Expenditure, receipts and borrowing

	£ billion		
	1995–96		1996–97
	1994 Budget	Estimated outturn	
General government expenditure	*301·8*	302·1	308·3
General government receipts	*278·7*	271·9	284·8
General government borrowing requirement	*23·1*	30·2	23·5
Public corporations' market and overseas borrowing	*–0·8*	–1·2	–1·1
Public sector borrowing requirement	**22·3**	**29·0**	**22·4**

[1] *On a cash basis. See Annex B to Chapter 4.*

[2] *Includes district council rates in Northern Ireland.*

[3] *Includes council tax.*

[4] *Includes interest and dividends, gross trading surpluses, rent, other financial transactions, and payments to the National Lottery Distribution Fund.*

[5] *Central government debt interest payments net of interest payments and dividend receipts from outside general government.*

[6] *General government expenditure excluding privatisation proceeds and lottery-financed spending and net of interest and dividend receipts.*

[7] *Lottery-financed spending, and interest and dividend receipts.*

Chart 1.3: General government expenditure (X) by function 1996–97

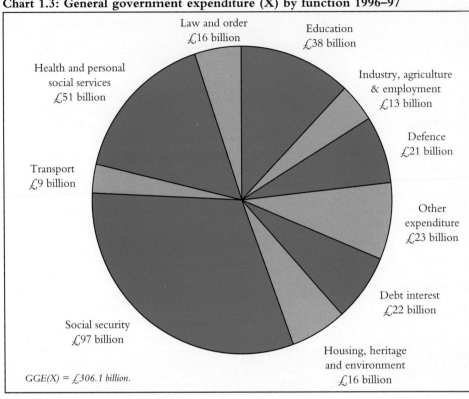

Law and order
£16 billion

Education
£38 billion

Health and personal
social services
£51 billion

Industry, agriculture
& employment
£13 billion

Defence
£21 billion

Transport
£9 billion

Other
expenditure
£23 billion

Debt interest
£22 billion

Social security
£97 billion

Housing, heritage
and environment
£16 billion

GGE(X) = £306.1 billion.

Chart 1.4: The financing of GGE(X) 1996–97

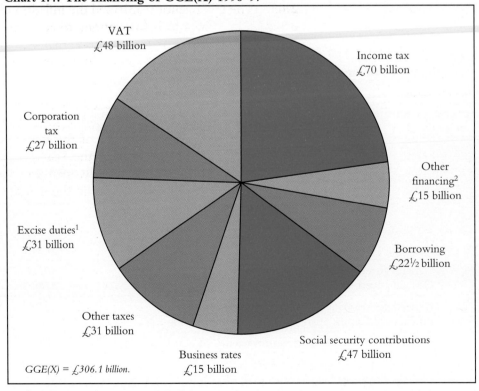

VAT
£48 billion

Income tax
£70 billion

Corporation
tax
£27 billion

Other
financing[2]
£15 billion

Excise duties[1]
£31 billion

Borrowing
£22½ billion

Other taxes
£31 billion

Social security contributions
£47 billion

Business rates
£15 billion

GGE(X) = £306.1 billion.

[1] *Excise duties on fuel, alcohol and tobacco.*

[2] *Other financing includes: public corporations' market and overseas borrowing, privatisation proceeds, gross trading surpluses, rent, other financial transactions, and payments to the National Lottery Distribution Fund net of lottery financed spending.*

2 The Medium-Term Financial Strategy

2.01 The objective of the Government's economic policy is to promote sustained economic growth and rising prosperity. This requires structural policies to improve the long-term performance of the economy and a stable macroeconomic environment. This chapter describes the macroeconomic policy framework. Monetary and fiscal policies are directed at maintaining low inflation on a permanent basis and sound public finances.

Inflation

2.02 Economies work most efficiently when inflation is low and stable. Since October 1992 the Government has set an explicit inflation objective: to keep underlying inflation (measured by the RPI excluding mortgage interest payments) within the range 1–4 per cent and to get down to the lower half of the range by the end of the present Parliament.

2.03 The Chancellor reaffirmed the inflation objective in June 1995, and also extended it. The aim is to continue to achieve underlying inflation of 2½ per cent or less beyond the end of this Parliament. Monetary policy will continue to be set consistently to achieve this target.

2.04 Since inflation targets have been set inflation has remained below 4 per cent for the longest continuous period for almost 50 years. Through a series of steps culminating in publication of the minutes of the Chancellor's monthly meetings with the Governor of the Bank of England, the monetary policy framework has become increasingly open over the last three years. As a result it has become one of the most open in the world.

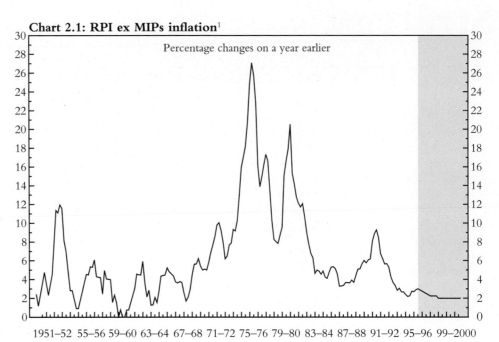

Chart 2.1: RPI ex MIPs inflation[1]

Percentage changes on a year earlier

1951–52 55–56 59–60 63–64 67–68 71–72 75–76 79–80 83–84 87–88 91–92 95–96 99–2000

[1] *Quarterly outturns until 1995 Q3; forecast from Table 3.5; projections (financial year averages) thereafter.*

Monetary policy

2.05   The role of monetary policy is to deliver permanently low inflation. Since monetary policy influences inflation with a lag, interest rate decisions are based on an assessment of the prospects for inflation up to two years ahead. This assessment is based on a wide range of information, including:

- **monetary and other financial indicators** including narrow and broad money, movements in the exchange rate and asset prices, and expectations about future inflation;

- **indicators of activity** including measures of the level of demand (for example measures of spare capacity, retail sales growth and labour shortages). The overall stance of fiscal policy is also taken into account;

- **indicators of costs**, in particular wage costs and material input prices (including commodity prices).

2.06   Interest rate decisions are not based solely on any one indicator, but on an overall assessment of all the relevant information concerning the prospects for inflation. As the framework is forward-looking, monetary policy responds to changes in cost and demand pressures which alter the outlook for inflation. Thus, the concern last year that the economy was growing at an unsustainably fast rate was one of the factors behind the increases in interest rates. Inflation forecasts are one useful way of summarising much of the information about inflation prospects. However, decisions are not based on a single point forecast but on an assessment of the risks and uncertainties surrounding the outlook for inflation.

2.07   Since the inflation target was first introduced the Government has explicitly acknowledged that events outside its control, such as a sharp movement in commodity prices, might temporarily take inflation away from the target level. The Government cannot predict how large these shocks might be, or whether they will be favourable or unfavourable. But the Government believes that, by setting interest rates consistently at the level judged necessary to achieve the inflation target of 2½ per cent or less, it should ensure inflation will remain in the range 1–4 per cent.

2.08   The Government has also set medium-term monitoring ranges for M0 and M4, although the information from these indicators is assessed alongside all the other data.

2.09   M0 growth has been above its medium-term monitoring range of 0–4 per cent since early 1993. In 1993 and 1994 rapid M0 growth was partly the result of the expected temporary effect of adjustment to lower interest rates. The persistence of strong M0 growth into 1995 has been more difficult to explain, and may suggest a structural change in M0's trend relative to GDP (see Chart 2.2).

Chart 2.2: Ratio of M0 to GDP

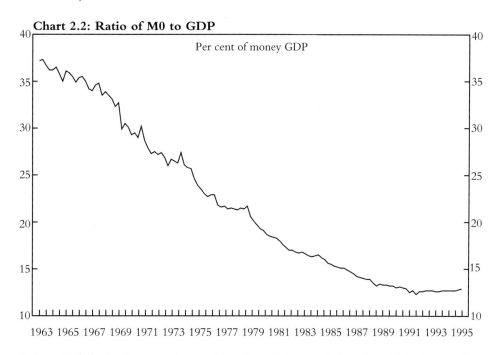

Per cent of money GDP

1963 1965 1967 1969 1971 1973 1975 1977 1979 1981 1983 1985 1987 1989 1991 1993 1995

2.10   While M4's growth rate has risen this year it is still within its medium-term monitoring range of 3–9 per cent. M4's trend relative to GDP has stabilised in recent years but, as Chart 2.3 shows, it has varied considerably in the past – in particular when financial markets were liberalised in the 1980s.

Chart 2.3: Ratio of M4 to GDP

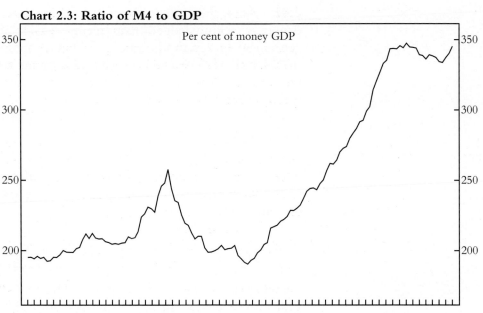

Per cent of money GDP

2.11   In view of the uncertainties about the trend in M0 and M4 relative to GDP, the Government has decided to leave the existing medium-term monitoring ranges unchanged. The Government will continue to keep the monitoring ranges under review.

Fiscal policy

2.12   The role of fiscal policy is to maintain sound public finances. The Government's fiscal objective is to bring the PSBR back towards balance over the medium term, and in particular to ensure that when the economy is on trend the public sector borrows no more than is required to finance its net capital spending.

2.13   The PSBR has fallen sharply in the past couple of years. Tight control of public spending is the key to its continued reduction, although the pace at which it declines will also depend on the path of the economy over the medium term. The spending plans and the tax policies announced in the Budget would, on the main projection set out in Chapters 3 and 4, bring the PSBR back to balance by 1999–2000.

2.14   A position of current balance, ie the public sector borrowing no more than needed to finance its net capital expenditure is projected to be reached in 1998–99.

2.15   As the PSBR returns towards balance, the general government financial deficit in 1996-97 is now expected to be close to the reference value of 3 per cent of GDP used in the European Union's excessive deficits procedure, and to fall substantially below that level in subsequent years. The ratio of gross general government debt to GDP remains below the reference value of 60 per cent throughout.

2.16   Since the November 1993 Budget the public sector accounts have made a clearer distinction between current and capital expenditure. The Government does not have a target for capital spending and the development of the private finance initiative changes significantly the balance between publicly financed current and capital spending. The development of resource accounts, as set out in the White Paper "Better Accounting for the Taxpayer's Money" (Cm 2929), will in due course provide a much better overall picture of the public finances, including the current/capital distinction.

2.17   National saving is now rising from the relatively low levels to which it fell in the recession of the early 1990s. Reducing the PSBR will contribute to a further increase in national saving, providing resources for investment and improving the long-run productive potential of the economy.

3 The economy: recent developments and prospects

Summary

World economy **3.01**   Growth has slowed this year in both North America and Europe. It is expected to average about 2½ per cent for the G7 as a whole in 1995, compared with 3 per cent in 1994, and is projected to continue at about 2½ per cent in 1996.

Activity **3.02**   Growth has moderated in the UK too, partly because of slower export growth. After rising by 4 per cent in 1994, GDP is likely to increase by around 2¾ per cent in 1995. Growth of 3 per cent is forecast for 1996.

Inflation **3.03**   Underlying RPI inflation was just under 3 per cent in October, compared with 2 per cent a year ago. Inflationary pressure has come mainly from higher import prices, reflecting the increase in commodity prices in 1994 and the depreciation of sterling early this year. This pressure has begun to ease, and inflation is expected to fall back to 2¼ per cent by the second quarter of 1997.

Labour market **3.04**   Employment has continued to rise, and labour force participation has also picked up recently as job prospects have improved further. The survey-based measure of unemployment has flattened off recently, but the claimant count has fallen by a further 150,000 so far this year, and in October was 710,000 below its peak in December 1992.

Current account **3.05**   The current account deficit has increased this year, mainly because net investment income has dropped back from its exceptionally high level of last year. A deficit of around £6½ billion is forecast for 1995, followed by a smaller deficit of around £5 billion in 1996.

Financial conditions **3.06**   The sterling index declined by about 5 per cent over the first three months of this year, but has ranged mainly between 83 and 85 since April. The forecast is based on the conventional assumption that sterling remains close to recent levels. Short-term interest rates have remained unchanged since February, while long rates have fallen. M0 growth has slowed, while M4 has accelerated, mainly because corporate borrowing has picked up.

Medium-term projections **3.07**   For the purpose of the medium-term fiscal projections, GDP is assumed to grow by around 2¾ per cent a year from 1997–98. Inflation as measured by the GDP deflator is assumed to fall from 2¾ per cent in 1996–97 to 2 per cent by 1999–2000.

The economy in the short term

World background

Activity **3.08** World output and trade increased sharply in 1994, but growth has slowed this year. This has been the pattern in most of the major seven economies (G7). In the US, GDP rose by 4 per cent in 1994, but growth then slowed sharply in the first half of 1995. This was partly a stock adjustment, and there was a strong pick-up in growth in the third quarter. Europe also slowed down in the first half of 1995 after the more rapid growth of last year. But in Japan recovery is not yet firmly established.

3.09 G7 growth is projected to be 2½ per cent in 1995, down from 3 per cent last year. It is forecast to continue at 2½ per cent in 1996. Growth rates within the G7 should start to converge in 1996 as Japan finally starts to recover. The US economy is forecast to grow by around 3¼ per cent in 1995 and slow to around 2½ per cent in 1996. Growth is also expected to average about 2½ per cent in Europe.

Table 3.1   The world economy

| | Percentage changes on a year earlier | | | |
| | | Forecast | | |
	1994	1995	1996	1997 H1
Major seven countries[1]				
Real GDP	3	2½	2½	2½
Domestic demand	3¼	2½	2¼	2¼
Industrial production	4¼	3¼	2½	2½
Consumer price inflation[2]	2¼	2½	2½	2½
World trade in manufactures	12	10½	8½	8½
UK export markets[3]	11	10½	8	8¼

[1] G7: US, Japan, Germany, France, Italy, UK and Canada.
[2] Final quarter of each period. For UK, RPI excluding mortgage interest payments.
[3] Other countries' imports of manufactures weighted according to their importance in UK exports.

World trade **3.10** The slowdown in the world economy in the first half of the year has brought a slowing in world trade growth from the rapid rates of 1994. Nevertheless, world trade is still expected to increase by 10½ per cent in 1995. It is forecast to grow at around 8½ per cent a year over the next 18 months, on the back of output growth at about trend rates in most industrial countries and continuing fast rates of growth in the emerging markets of Southeast Asia. UK export markets are likely to grow slightly slower than world trade as a whole because intra-regional trade in Southeast Asia is expected to be particularly buoyant.

Chart 3.1: G7 GDP and world trade

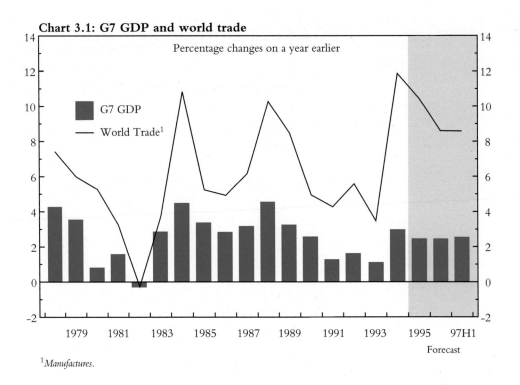

¹*Manufactures.*

Commodity prices **3.11** Non-oil commodity prices rose sharply in 1994, because of the combined effect of strong world trade, supply shortages and speculative pressures. But they fell back in the early months of 1995 and, despite a slight pick up recently, are not expected to be a source of renewed inflationary pressure. Brent oil prices have also fallen back, from a peak of around $20 a barrel in April, to around $16½ a barrel. The forecast assumes that oil prices remain close to this level.

Chart 3.2: Non-oil commodity prices¹

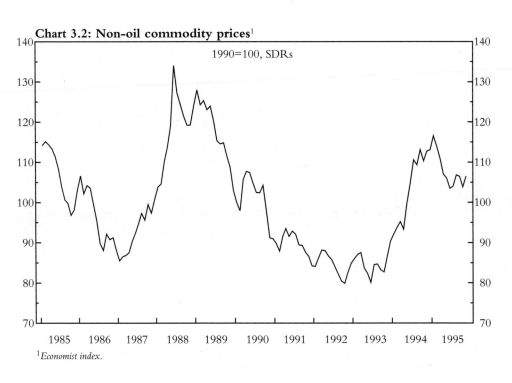

¹*Economist index.*

Inflation **3.12** The pick-up in G7 consumer price inflation looks to have been short-lived. Inflation has already fallen back in the US, and has turned out lower than expected in Germany (in part reflecting the rebasing of the index). In Japan, prices are broadly flat. With few cost-push pressures in the pipeline, output growth at trend rates, and probably still some spare capacity in aggregate, the outlook for inflation is benign. G7 inflation is forecast to remain at around 2½ per cent.

Interest rates **3.13** In the US, the Federal Reserve began to tighten policy in February 1994, increasing the Federal Funds rate by 3 percentage points by February this year. It then cut rates by a ¼ percentage point in July. The Bundesbank cut its discount rate to 3½ per cent in August, the twelfth cut since the peak of 8¾ per cent in September 1992. The Bank of Japan cut its discount rate to a record low of ½ per cent in September in response to the continued weakness of the Japanese economy. With renewed confidence that inflation will remain low, world long-term rates have generally fallen back in 1995, reversing most of the sharp increase last year.

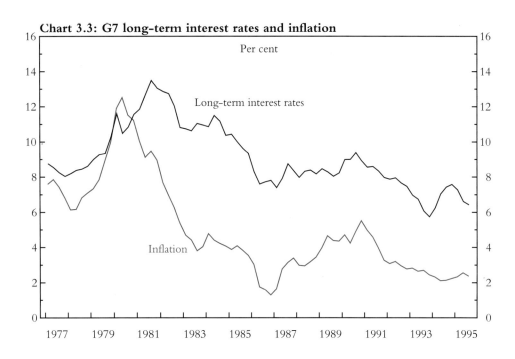

Chart 3.3: G7 long-term interest rates and inflation

Demand and output

Recent developments   **3.14**   Growth in the UK has also moderated this year. After increasing by 4 per cent in 1994, GDP grew at an annual rate of around 2 per cent over the first three quarters of 1995. However, because of the rapid growth through last year, GDP is still likely to increase by about 2¾ per cent between 1994 and 1995. Manufacturing output growth has slowed and construction output has fallen. In contrast, the trend in output of services has continued fairly steadily upwards, with the output of the transport and communication industries rising especially fast.

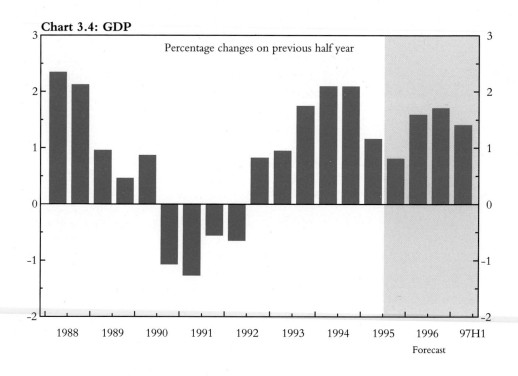

Chart 3.4: GDP

Percentage changes on previous half year

1988   1989   1990   1991   1992   1993   1994   1995   1996   97H1

Forecast

3.15   Exports of goods rose by over 10 per cent in 1994, the largest increase for over 20 years. They flattened off in the first half of this year as world trade decelerated; and this is probably the main reason for the slower rise in manufacturing output. Consumers' expenditure has hardly slowed, on the latest data, despite the tightening of fiscal and monetary policies. Manufacturing investment in plant and machinery has picked up strongly. But, with construction comparatively weak, fixed investment in total is likely to grow more slowly this year. The growth of government consumption has also slowed.

Prospects   **3.16**   Exports now appear to be picking up again. They remain highly profitable, and are likely to increase substantially next year if world demand continues to expand. Consumer demand may also strengthen as real disposable incomes rise more quickly. Business surveys suggest that business investment could rise quite strongly, but housing investment may remain weak for some time. Direct public sector investment is falling, but offsetting increases in private investment are expected under the Private Finance Initiative. Stockbuilding, which has been quite high this year, could make a small negative contribution to growth next year.

3.17 With this outlook for the components of demand, GDP growth is expected to pick up from recent rates of around 2 per cent to 3¼ per cent through 1996. This would imply an increase in GDP of 3 per cent in 1996 as a whole.

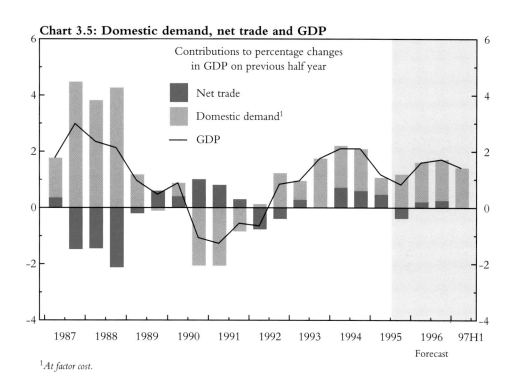

Chart 3.5: Domestic demand, net trade and GDP

Contributions to percentage changes in GDP on previous half year

Net trade
Domestic demand¹
— GDP

Forecast

¹At factor cost.

Personal sector and the housing market

Consumers' expenditure

3.18 Consumers' expenditure has risen by 2¼ per cent at an annual rate over the first three quarters of this year, which is similar to its rate of increase during the course of last year. Retail sales have been broadly flat this year, and most of the growth in consumer spending has been on services (which are not included in retail sales). Real personal disposable income has risen more quickly this year, partly because of higher dividend payments. The saving ratio, which had fallen from 12¼ per cent in 1992 to 9¾ per cent in 1994¹, does not appear to have changed substantially this year.

---

¹ For an explanation of the basis of this estimate, see footnote 1 to Table 3.8.

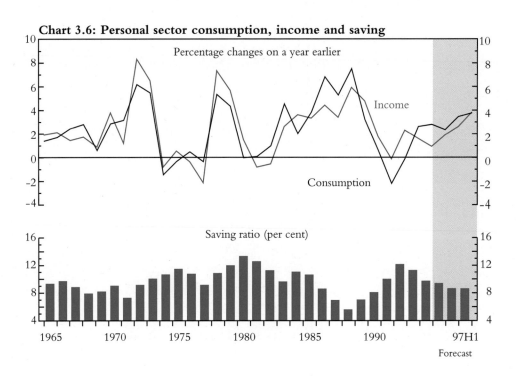

Chart 3.6: Personal sector consumption, income and saving

3.19   Survey evidence suggests that consumer confidence has been on a slight upward trend in recent months, but consumers remain wary about making major purchases. Despite the falls in 1993 and 1994, the saving ratio is still fairly high given the historically low rate of inflation, and households are accumulating substantial net financial assets. Their debt–income ratio, which rose steeply during the 1980s, has fallen slightly since 1991 and debt servicing costs have been sharply reduced as a result of lower interest rates. Saving for personal pensions, comparatively high real interest rates, job insecurity and the weakness of the housing market all suggest that the saving ratio could remain quite high for a time, and the forecast assumes only a comparatively small further fall. Real personal disposable income and consumption are forecast to rise by 2 and 2¼ per cent respectively in 1995. Real incomes are projected to rise by 2¾ per cent next year, partly because taxes are being reduced, and consumers' expenditure is forecast to grow by 3½ per cent.

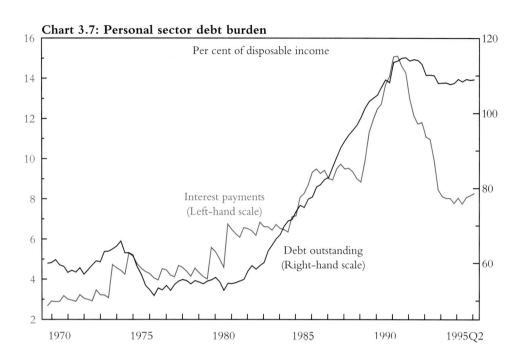

Chart 3.7: Personal sector debt burden

Housing market

3.20 House prices are 2 per cent lower than at the start of the year, while turnover is over 13 per cent lower. Demand and supply may still be adjusting to some extent to the boom in the late 1980s. In addition, some potential house buyers, especially first time buyers, may have been delaying moves until after the Budget. However, the latest data indicate that house prices may have reached the bottom of their cycle. The Department of the Environment index rose in the second quarter, and was unchanged in the third quarter; the Halifax index has now risen for three months in succession; and although the Nationwide index fell in October, it is still above the level in June. Turnover also appears to have stabilised recently.

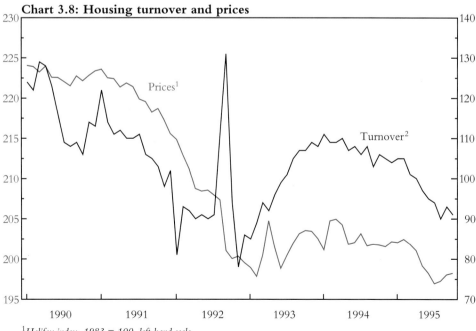

Chart 3.8: Housing turnover and prices

[1]Halifax index, 1983 = 100, left-hand scale.
[2]Particulars delivered, thousands, right-hand scale.

3.21 A modest housing market recovery is projected for 1996, encouraged by higher real income growth, low mortgage rates, an historically low house price-earnings ratio, and an increasing number of first-time buyers. To the extent that there is still pent up supply in the market, the recovery may be reflected at first more in turnover than prices, which are forecast to rise only slowly next year.

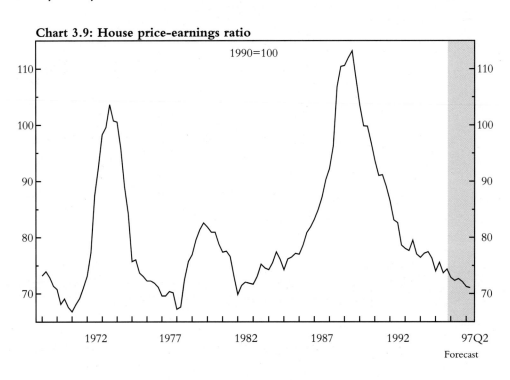

Chart 3.9: House price-earnings ratio

Private housing investment

3.22 Housing completions have been on an upward trend; but this reflects the increase in starts last year, and with starts recently falling short of completions, the number of houses under construction has been falling. Nevertheless private housing investment (which includes improvements, maintenance and net purchases of land and existing buildings as well as new housebuilding) is projected to rise by 3¼ per cent in 1996.

Financial position

3.23 With no large change in either the saving or investment ratios, the personal sector is expected to maintain a significant financial surplus. At around 3 per cent of income, it would be close to the average of the last 30 years.

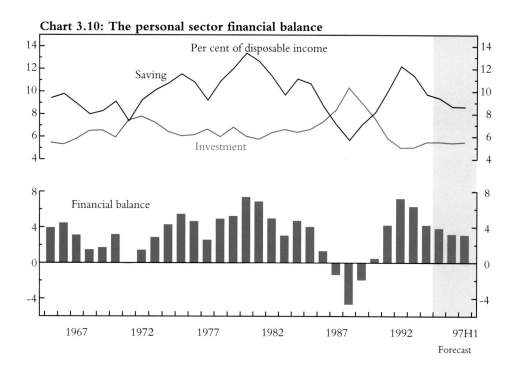

Chart 3.10: The personal sector financial balance

Corporate sector and investment

Profits   **3.24**   Profits of industrial and commercial have increased by over one third over the past three years. Their share in GDP has risen from 12½ per cent in 1992 to 14½ per cent in the first three quarters of 1995, and the real rate of return on capital is approaching levels last seen in the late 1980s. With generally strong balance sheets and easy access to external finance, it is not surprising that the October CBI survey indicates that relatively few firms regard availability of finance as a major constraint on investment.

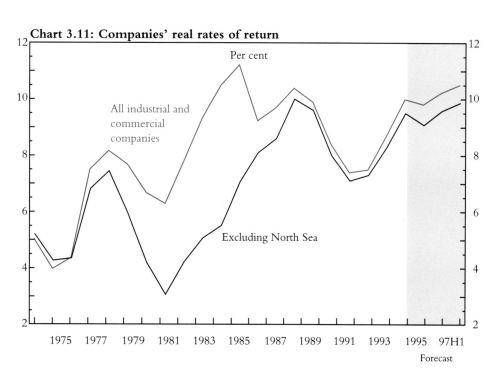

Chart 3.11: Companies' real rates of return

Business investment   **3.25**   Business investment has fluctuated from quarter to quarter, but appears to have been on a rising trend since the beginning of last year. The aggregate figures conceal very different movements in different sectors. Manufacturing investment turned up at the beginning of 1994, and by the third quarter of this year was over 20 per cent higher than at its trough. Investment by the privatised utilities (gas, electricity and water) was heavy from 1991 to 1993, but has now passed its peak. North Sea investment has also fallen back from high levels in the early 1990s. Other business investment (mainly in services) has been rising since the start of 1994.

3.26   Surveys of manufacturers' intentions suggest that there is still a good deal of planned investment in the pipeline. Manufacturing capacity utilisation is still at a high level, and according to the CBI survey the need to increase capacity is an increasingly important incentive to invest. Manufacturing investment is forecast to increase by over 10 per cent both this year and in 1996. The British Chambers of Commerce survey suggests that investment intentions are also quite high in services. However, construction orders remain low, and investment in plant and machinery is likely to be more buoyant than investment in buildings.

3.27   The prospect is for a substantial rise in business investment in total, but not a boom of late 1980s' proportions. An increase of 3¼ per cent is forecast for this year, and 9 per cent for 1996.

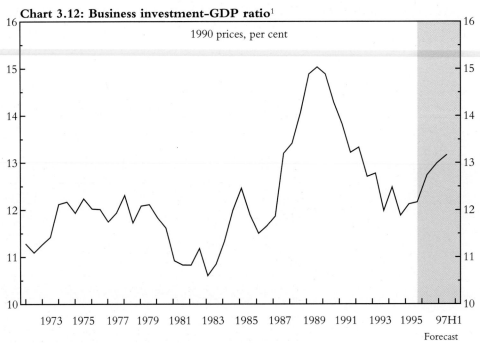

Chart 3.12: Business investment–GDP ratio[1]

1990 prices, per cent

[1] *Business investment includes public corporations (except National Health Trust hospitals) and investment under the Private Finance Initiative.*

Whole economy investment

3.28 The forecast of business investment takes full account of the substantial investment planned under the Private Finance Initiative, which offsets planned reductions in directly financed public investment. With, in addition, only modest increases in investment in housing and land projected over the next 18 months, investment for the economy as a whole is likely to increase significantly less than business investment. Even so, it is forecast to rise by over 4 per cent in 1996.

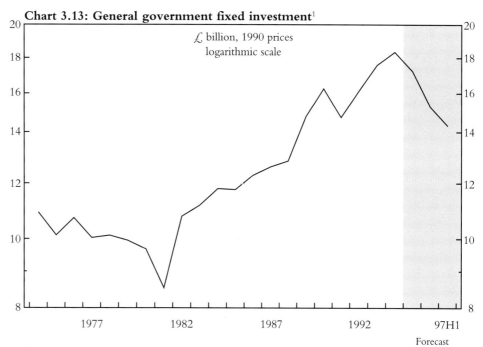

Chart 3.13: General government fixed investment¹

£ billion, 1990 prices
logarithmic scale

Forecast

¹ *Excludes capital expenditure under the Private Finance Initiative. First half of 1997 is at an annual rate.*

Table 3.2   Gross domestic fixed capital formation

| | Percentage changes on a year earlier | | | |
| | | Forecast | | |
	1994	1995	1996	1997 H1
Business¹	1½	3¼	9	6¾
Private dwellings and land²	6½	1	3¼	4¼
General government³	4¼	−6	−11	−9
Whole economy	3	1	4¼	3¾

¹ *Includes public corporations (except National Health Trust hospitals) and investment under the Private Finance Initiative.*
² *Includes net purchases of land and existing buildings for the whole economy.*
³ *Excludes net purchases of land and existing buildings; includes National Health Trust hospitals.*

Stockbuilding

3.29 Stockbuilding increased sharply in the third quarter of 1995 and has been high on average for the last four quarters. The increase in stocks has been large in manufacturing and the retail trade, and the ratio of total stocks to GDP has risen against its long-term downward trend. A lower rate of stockbuilding may temporarily reduce output growth, but this effect is expected to be short-lived.

31

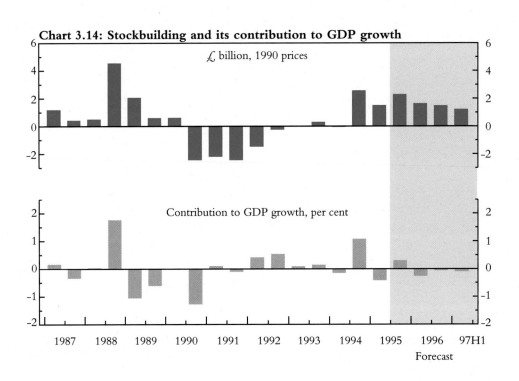

Chart 3.14: Stockbuilding and its contribution to GDP growth

£ billion, 1990 prices

Contribution to GDP growth, per cent

Forecast

Financial balance **3.30** Industrial and commercial companies remain in substantial financial surplus. However, the surplus is projected to fall from 2 per cent of GDP in 1994 to virtually zero in 1996, under the twin influences of strong investment and lower saving.

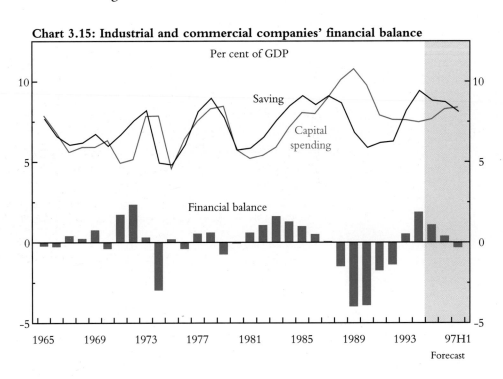

Chart 3.15: Industrial and commercial companies' financial balance

Per cent of GDP

Saving

Capital spending

Financial balance

Forecast

Trade and the balance of payments

Competitiveness   **3.31**   Most measures of competitiveness continue to show the UK in a strong position. Import prices have risen far more than domestic producer prices so far this year, which implies a further improvement in the price competitiveness of domestically produced goods relative to imports. Cost competitiveness also benefited from the weakness of sterling early this year.

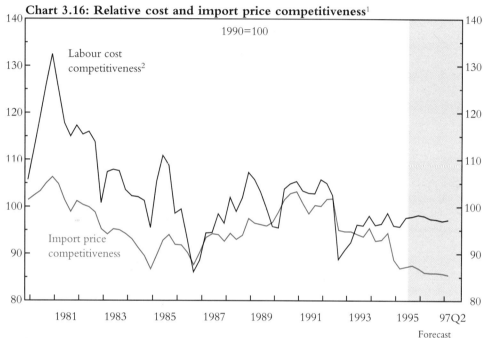

Chart 3.16: Relative cost and import price competitiveness[1]

1990=100

Labour cost competitiveness[2]

Import price competitiveness

1981   1983   1985   1987   1989   1991   1993   1995   97Q2

Forecast

[1] A fall means competitiveness has improved.
[2] Against major 15 industrial countries.

3.32   The position on export price competitiveness does not appear so strong. However, exports are very profitable. When sterling depreciated early this year, exporters maintained their prices in foreign currency terms, again taking the benefit in the form of higher profit margins. This pattern is consistent with the export prices of standard products being determined on world markets, rather than being set by UK firms. High profit margins will increase the incentive to supply overseas markets. In the longer term it will also encourage investment to increase capacity, and there are already signs of this happening in manufacturing.

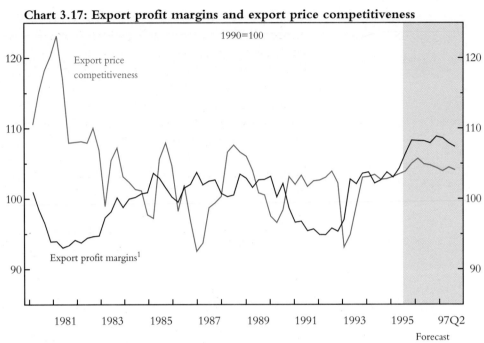

Chart 3.17: Export profit margins and export price competitiveness

1990=100

^{1}Ratio of manufacturing export prices to estimated manufacturing costs.

Export volumes
3.33 After rising by 10 per cent in 1994, the volume of non-oil exports of goods was little changed in the first half of this year. The slowdown in the world economy partly accounts for this flattening off. Delivery times may also have lengthened. But, with business surveys suggesting a more buoyant picture, it is conceivable that the volume of exports has been understated. Third-quarter data suggest that exports have started to pick up again. Over the next 18 months, exports of manufactures are projected broadly to maintain their market share.

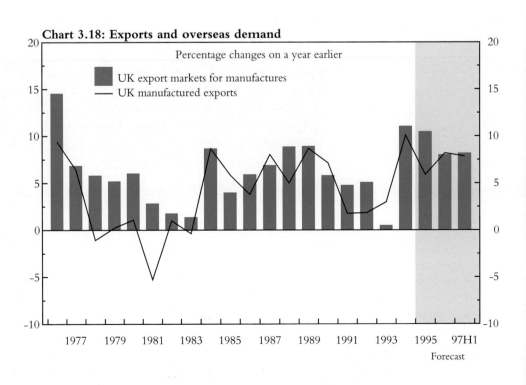

Chart 3.18: Exports and overseas demand

Percentage changes on a year earlier

■ UK export markets for manufactures
— UK manufactured exports

Import volumes   **3.34**   Over the past year and a half, non-oil import volumes have moved erratically. This year they fell in the first quarter, picked up in the second and continued rising into the third quarter. Despite the recent increases, the current level of imports does not appear unusually high in relation to demand. With growing investment and high stockbuilding, capital and intermediate goods imports have been relatively strong, while imports of consumer goods have been relatively weak. Over the next 18 months, imports are projected to rise rather faster than final expenditure, but less so than typically in the past because of the strong competitive position of UK manufacturers. In the longer term the build-up of UK manufacturing capacity may also tend to reduce import growth through greater import substitution.

Chart 3.19: Imports and total final expenditure

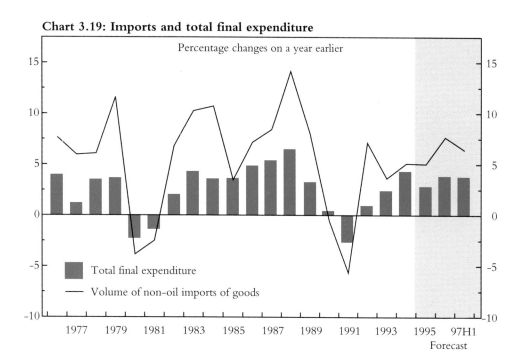

Trade prices   **3.35**   Following sterling's depreciation early this year, both export and import prices increased sharply. With import prices rising more than export prices, the terms of trade deteriorated further. However, the growth of export and particularly import prices has moderated recently, and part of the deterioration in the terms of trade has already been reversed. Assuming a constant exchange rate and no marked change in commodity prices, little change in the terms of trade is projected over the next 18 months.

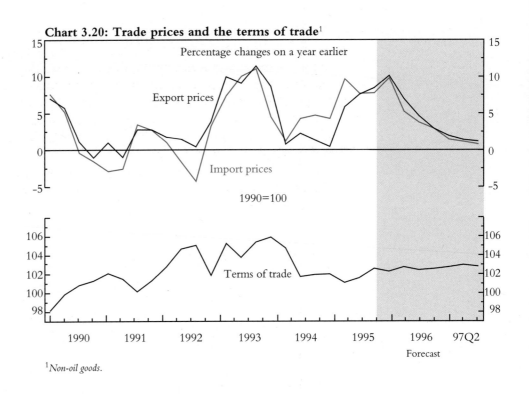

Chart 3.20: Trade prices and the terms of trade[1]

Percentage changes on a year earlier

1990=100

Forecast

[1] *Non-oil goods.*

Table 3.3 Non-oil visible trade

	Percentage changes on a year earlier					£ billion
	Volumes		Prices[1]			Non-oil visible balance
	Exports	Imports	Exports	Imports	Terms of trade[2]	
1994	10	5	1¼	3½	−2¼	−14¾
Forecast						
1995	6½	5	8	8¾	−¾	−15¾
1996	8¼	7¾	4	3¼	¾	−15½
1997 H1	7½	6½	1¼	1	¼	−14¾[3]

[1] *Average value indices.*
[2] *Ratio of export to import prices.*
[3] *At an annual rate.*

Visible balance   **3.36**   The non-oil visible deficit increased by almost £½ billion between the second half of last year and the first half of 1995. This is more than fully explained by the deterioration in the terms of trade; the balance improved in volume terms. The deficit is projected to fall slightly next year, as export volumes recover and the terms of trade are a little higher.

Oil   **3.37**   The oil surplus has increased since the end of last year, but fell back a little in the second quarter, and fell further during the summer because of maintenance work in the North Sea. Oil production has since picked up again, and the oil surplus is likely to increase as a result.

Invisibles   **3.38**   The surplus on invisibles quadrupled last year to £9¾ billion, its highest level relative to GDP since 1987, due mainly to higher net investment income. There were, however, a number of exceptional factors underlying this increase, for example a sharp fall in the profits of overseas financial institutions operating in the UK and unusually high net earnings from interest rate swaps. A fall-back in 1995 was expected, therefore, as these exceptional factors unwound. This fall was exacerbated by the Barings losses in the first half of 1995, and a number of other factors, such as a small increase in UK interest rates relative to those overseas. In the event, the invisibles surplus fell to an annual rate of £4¾ billion in the first half of this year. It is projected to remain at about this level over the next year and a half.

Table 3.4   The current account[1]

	Manufactures	Oil	Other	Total visibles	Invisibles	Current balance
			£ billion			
1993	−8¼	2½	−7¾	−13½	2¼	−11
1994	−7½	4	−7¼	−10¾	9¾	−¾
Forecast						
1995	−8¾	4½	−7	−11½	4¾	−6½
1996	−9½	5¼	−6¼	−10¼	5¼	−5
1997 H1[2]	−9	5½	−5¾	−9¼	5	−4¼

[1] *The estimate of the current account deficit for 1994 takes account of revisions to visible and invisible trade statistics since the last CSO Balance of Payments release on 22 September (see footnote 1 to Table 3.8).*
[2] *At an annual rate.*

Current account   **3.39**   A current account deficit of about £6½ billion is expected in 1995, £5¾ billion higher than in 1994. Almost all of this increase is accounted for by the fall-back in net investment income. The deficit is projected to narrow by £1½ billion in 1996, largely as a result of a lower deficit on visible trade. The projected deficits in 1995 and 1996 are relatively small at ¾−1 per cent of GDP.

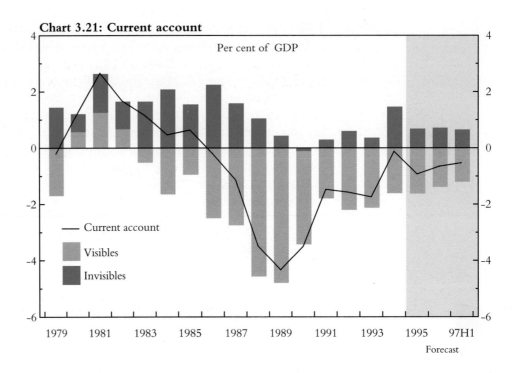

Chart 3.21: Current account

Pattern of financial balances

3.40   With the current account expected to remain in small deficit, the projected fall in the private sector financial surplus closely mirrors the fall in the public sector deficit. The fall in the private sector financial surplus, from 6½ per cent of GDP in 1994 to 2½ per cent in 1996, comes largely through a lower corporate sector surplus.

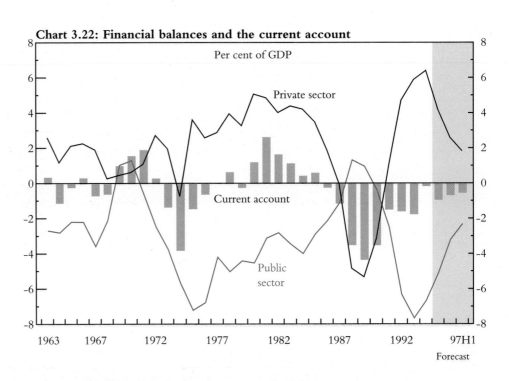

Chart 3.22: Financial balances and the current account

Labour market

Employment

3.41   Employment continues to rise. The employer survey measure shows an increase of 510,000 since its trough at the end of 1992, while the Labour Force Survey (LFS) measure has risen by 650,000 over a similar period.[1] The employer survey shows employment growth slowing recently, with an increase of 80,000 in the first half of 1995, compared with 220,000 in the second half of last year. But the LFS measure shows little deceleration, with an increase of over 160,000 between the winter and summer, not much less than the increase in the previous half year.

Chart 3.23: Employment and unemployment

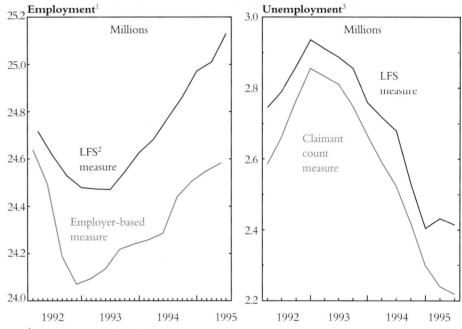

[1] GB employees plus self-employed.
[2] LFS data recorded against central month of each LFS quarter.
[3] GB. Time periods relate to LFS quarters: Q1-December to February (winter); Q2-March to May (Spring); etc.

Productivity

3.42   Productivity rose less rapidly in the first half of this year, probably reflecting a lag in the adjustment of employment to lower output growth. Non-oil output per person employed rose at an annual rate of 1½ per cent, compared with 2¾ per cent in 1994. Over the next 18 months, non-oil productivity is projected to rise at around its trend rate. Manufacturing productivity has also slowed, for a similar reason, but is expected to pick up next year as output picks up.

---

[1] Figures for employment relate to employees plus self-employed in Great Britain.

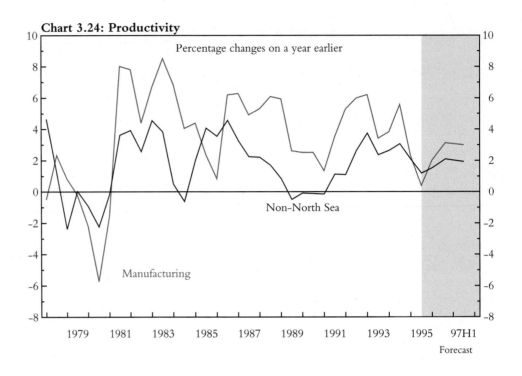

Chart 3.24: Productivity

Percentage changes on a year earlier

Non–North Sea

Manufacturing

1979   1981   1983   1985   1987   1989   1991   1993   1995   97H1

Forecast

Unemployment   **3.43**   UK claimant unemployment is now over 710,000 below its end–1992 peak. The monthly rate of decline has tended to slow for most of this year. It averaged around 12,000 a month in July to October, against an average last year of 30,000 a month. The LFS measure of unemployment in Great Britain has also fallen substantially and is now over 520,000 less than in winter 1992/93. On either measure, the unemployment rate has declined to 8–8½ per cent from 10½ per cent around end–1992.

Labour force   **3.44**   However, the LFS measure of unemployment has changed relatively little since last winter. As employment has continued to rise, this implies a substantial increase in the labour force – the number of people either in or actively seeking work. According to the LFS, the number of economically active people in Great Britain, which had fallen by over 110,000 between winter 1992/93 (when unemployment peaked) and winter 1994/95, has since risen by over 140,000. Some of this rise is accounted for by demographic trends (more people of working age), but most is accounted for by a rising participation rate (a higher proportion of people in or seeking work). Participation had been falling because of increasing numbers of students and 'discouraged workers', but is now rising, partly because more people are being attracted into the labour force by better job prospects.

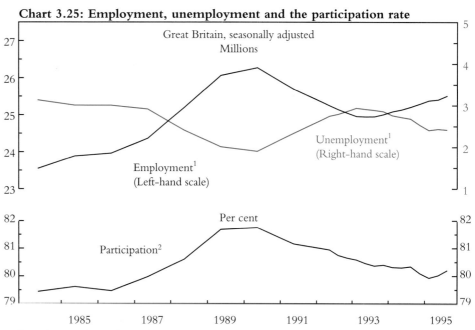

Chart 3.25: Employment, unemployment and the participation rate

[1]LFS data. Employment figures relate to total.
[2]LFS employment plus unemployment as a percentage of the population of working age.

Financial developments

Sterling **3.45** Sterling's exchange rate index, which measures the sterling exchange rate against a basket of currencies, fell by about 5 per cent in the first three months of the year, but has ranged mainly between 83 and 85 since April. During the year, sterling has traded in a fairly narrow range against the dollar but has fallen against the Deutschmark and the French Franc. Sterling lost ground against the Yen in the first half of the year but has since recovered.

Chart 3.26: Sterling effective exchange rate index

1990=100

Interest rates   **3.46**   Since the last Budget, base rates have been raised twice (by ½ percentage point in both December and February) to 6¾ per cent. Mortgage rates have, however, barely increased, reflecting competition in the mortgage market.

Long rates   **3.47**   UK long rates have declined gradually since the beginning of the year, largely reflecting international developments. Yields on ten year gilts were around 7¾ per cent in mid–November, down from 8¾ per cent in January. UK long rates have not fallen as much as those in the US and the differential has widened; but the differential against German rates has remained broadly constant for most of the year. Inflation expectations implied by gilts yields have declined a little since the end of 1994.

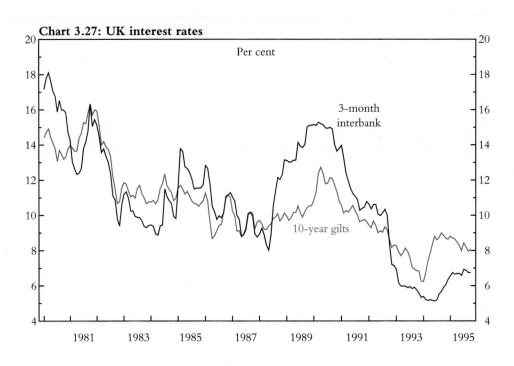

Chart 3.27: UK interest rates

Per cent

3-month interbank

10-year gilts

Asset prices   **3.48**   House prices appear to have stabilised following the falls during the first half of 1995. In the commercial property market too, there are signs that the recent falls in capital and rental values may soon be at an end. Equity prices have risen sharply during 1995, and the FT-SE All-Share index has risen by 17 per cent since last December.

Monetary aggregates   **3.49**   The annual growth rate of M0, 5·2 per cent in October, is still high. Rapid M0 growth during 1993 and 1994 was probably a result of continuing adjustment to falling interest rates. The persistence of strong growth in 1995 has been more difficult to explain, and may suggest a structural change in its trend relative to GDP, perhaps due to a slowdown in financial innovation and an adjustment to lower inflation.

3.50   The annual growth rate of M4 was 8·7 per cent in October, close to the top of its medium-term monitoring range. M4 lending – bank and building society lending to the UK private sector – has strengthened over the last year. Although lending for house purchase declined during the first three quarters, lending to industrial and commercial companies and other financial institutions has been strong for most of the year.

Chart 3.28: Monetary growth

Inflation

3.51   Inflation since June has been broadly in line with the Summer Economic Forecast. The 12–month rate of increase in the RPI excluding mortgage interest payments (MIPs) was 2·9 per cent in October, compared with 2 per cent a year ago. Producer output prices[1] have been decelerating since April, and the 3-month annualised rate of increase fell sharply in October to 4 per cent. Most of the increase in retail price inflation has been in goods, reflecting the increase in producer output prices; services inflation, which is more closely related to earnings growth, remains subdued.

Import costs   **3.52**   The main force pushing up goods prices has been higher import costs, arising from the sharp rise in commodity prices last year and the weakness of sterling earlier this year. In the first quarter, import prices were almost 10 per cent higher than a year before, but they have since slowed considerably as commodity prices have fallen back, and have been virtually unchanged since May. This has been reflected in the deceleration of producer input prices. The 3-month annualised rate of increase has fallen from a peak of over 16 per cent in March to just 1½ per cent in October.

Chart 3.29: Retail and import price inflation[1]

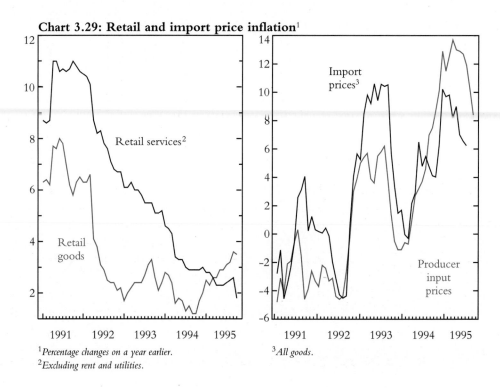

[1]*Percentage changes on a year earlier.*
[2]*Excluding rent and utilities.*
[3]*All goods.*

---

[1] *All references to producer input and output prices exclude the food, beverages, tobacco and petroleum industries.*

Earnings   **3.53**   Pay settlements have picked up very slightly recently, but earnings growth remains low, suggesting a decreasing contribution from overtime, grading increments and bonuses. This is probably partly related to the slowdown in output growth, although it may also partly reflect new working practices which have reduced increments and allowances. The underlying rate of increase in average earnings for the economy as a whole was just 3¼ per cent in the third quarter. This is close to the rate of increase recorded in autumn 1993, which in turn was the lowest since 1967.

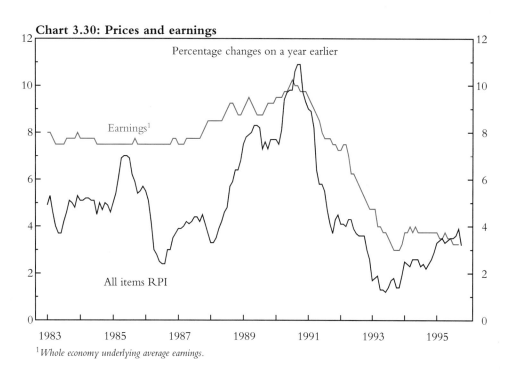

Chart 3.30: Prices and earnings

¹ *Whole economy underlying average earnings.*

Manufacturing sector   **3.54**   With capacity utilisation in manufacturing at high levels, manufacturers were able to improve margins earlier in the recovery. But as manufacturing output has slowed, pressure on prices from this source has eased. Therefore, movements in prices this year largely reflect changes in costs. The CBI price expectations balance, which is a good leading indicator of producer output prices, peaked in February, and has recently been at its lowest level since the middle of 1994. The Chartered Institute of Purchasing and Supply survey also shows inflationary pressures in manufacturing easing.

Retail sector   **3.55**   In retailing, the relative weakness of consumer demand has given firms little opportunity to raise margins. Competition remains fierce, as evidenced by recent attempts to end collective agreements in book retailing and pharmaceuticals. Although consumer demand is expected to pick up in 1996, a large rebound in retailers' margins seems unlikely in these circumstances.

Prospects **3.56** With external cost pressures easing and output still below trend, inflation may now be close to its peak. From 3 per cent in the last quarter of this year, RPI excluding MIPs inflation is forecast to fall back to 2¼ per cent by the second quarter of 1997. The forecast excludes any possible effect on measured inflation from electricity rebates associated with the flotation of the National Grid.

Table 3.5   Retail and producer output price inflation

| | Percentage changes on a year earlier | | | | |
| | | Forecast | | | |
	1994 Q4	1995 Q4	1996 Q2	1996 Q4	1997 Q2
RPI excluding MIPs[1]	2¼	3	2¾	2½	2¼
Producer output prices[2]	2½	4½	3	2	1¾

[1] *Excludes any possible effect on measured inflation from electricity rebates associated with the flotation of the National Grid.*
[2] *Excluding the food, beverages, tobacco and petroleum industries.*

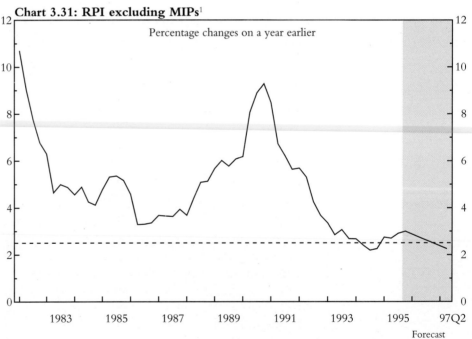

Chart 3.31: RPI excluding MIPs[1]

Percentage changes on a year earlier

[1]*Outturns until 1995Q3; forecast for 1995Q4, 1996Q2, 1996Q4 and 1997Q2.*

GDP deflator **3.57** The GDP deflator has been rising more slowly than the RPI excluding MIPs because of the deterioration in the terms of trade. With the terms of trade recovering slightly, it is projected to rise marginally faster than the RPI in 1996–97.

Risks and uncertainties

3.58   All forecasts are subject to risks and uncertainties. Average errors from past forecasts, shown in Table 3.8, are one illustration of their possible extent. Errors usually increase the further ahead the forecast looks. Obviously, errors on any individual forecast may be larger or smaller than the average.

3.59   The forecasts of GDP growth and inflation for this year are little changed from the Summer Economic Forecast. Growth is expected to be ½ percentage point lower than in the last Budget forecast, while RPI excluding MIPs inflation is ½ percentage point higher, partly due to the weakness of sterling early this year. The forecast of the current account deficit for this year has been revised up since the summer, mainly because the terms of trade and export volumes have both been lower than expected. The PSBR for the current financial year is now expected to be £5½ billion higher than forecast in the summer.

Table 3.6   Comparison with earlier forecasts

		Percentage changes on a year earlier unless otherwise stated		
		1994 Budget	1995 Summer Economic Forecast	1995 Budget
Gross domestic product	1995	3¼	3	2¾
	1996	–	2¾	3
RPI excluding mortgage interest payments	1995 Q4	2½	3	3
	1996 Q4	–	2½	2½
Current account (£ billion)	1995	−3½	−2	−6½
	1996	–	−1	−5
PSBR (£ billion)	1995–96	21½	23½	29
	1996–97	13	16	22½

The Panel of Independent Forecasters

3.60   Forecast uncertainties can also be illustrated by the range of views of members of the Panel of Independent Forecasters. For example, the Panel's forecasts of inflation at the end of 1996 range from 1¾ to 3¼ per cent. The forecasts of growth in 1996, however, cover a relatively narrow range of 2½ to 3 per cent. The Budget forecast of growth is the same as the Panel average for 1995, but at the upper end of the range for 1996. The Budget forecast of inflation for end-1995 and 1996 is the same as the Panel average. The Panel's views are set out in more detail in Annex B.

Table 3.7   Budget and Independent Panel[1] forecasts

	Percentage changes on a year earlier unless otherwise stated					
	1995			1996		
	Budget	Independent Panel		Budget	Independent Panel	
		Average	Range		Average	Range
Gross domestic product	2¾	2¾	2½ to 2¾	3	2¾	2½ to 3
RPI excluding mortgage interest payments (Q4)	3	3	2½ to 3¼	2½	2½	1¾ to 3¼
Current account (£ billion)	−6½	−6	−9 to −3	−5	−3¾	−9½ to 1½
PSBR (financial year, £ billion)	29	27½	25¼ to 30	22½	22	20¼ to 26

[1] *Submitted to the Chancellor of the Exchequer on 2 November; see Annex B for further details.*

Table 3.8   Summary of short-term economic prospects[1]

| | Percentage changes on a year earlier unless otherwise stated | | | |
	1994	Forecast 1995	Forecast 1996	Average errors from past forecasts[3]
Expenditure at constant prices[2]				
Domestic demand	3	2	2¾	1¾
Consumers' expenditure	2¾	2¼	3½	1¾
General government consumption	2	¾	¼	1¼
Fixed investment	3	1	4¼	3½
Change in stockbuilding[4]	½	¼	−¼	½
Exports of goods and services	9	5¾	7¼	2
Imports of goods and services	5¼	3¾	6¾	3
Gross domestic product	4	2¾	3	1½
Non-North Sea GDP	3½	2½	2¾	1½
Manufacturing output	4¼	2	2½	1¾
Balance of payments current account				
£ billion	−¾	−6½	−5	7¼
per cent of GDP	−¼	−1	−¾	1
Inflation				
RPI excluding mortgage interest payments (fourth quarter)	2¼	3	2½	1
Producer output prices (fourth quarter)[5]	2½	4½	2	1
GDP deflator at market prices (financial year)	2	2¾	2¾	1½
Money GDP at market prices (financial year)				
£ billion	678	712	754	
percentage change	6	5	6	2
PSBR (financial year)				
£ billion	36	29	22½	11
per cent of GDP	5¼	4	3	1½

[1] Data in this chapter are consistent with the output, income and expenditure estimates and other series for the period to the third quarter of 1995 released by the Central Statistical Office (CSO) on 20 November 1995. The CSO will not be publishing full national accounts estimates until 21 December 1995, but revisions to available data have been carried through by the Treasury to further series, such as personal saving, real incomes and the current account.
[2] Further detail on GDP and its components is given in Annex A.
[3] Average absolute error in autumn forecasts over past ten years: they apply to forecasts for 1996 unless otherwise indicated.
[4] Per cent of GDP.
[5] Excluding food, beverages, tobacco and petroleum industries.

The economy in the medium term

3.61   This section presents illustrative projections for output growth and inflation up to 2000–01 which form the basis of the medium-term fiscal projections in Chapter 4. The illustrative projections are set out in Table 3.9.

Table 3.9   Output growth and inflation[1]

	Percentage changes on previous financial year					
	1995–96	1996–97	1997–98	1998–99	1999–2000	2000-01
Output (GDP)						
Non-North Sea	2¼	3	3	2¾	2¾	2¾
Total	2¼	3	3	2¾	2¾	2¾
Prices						
GDP deflator	2¾	2¾	2½	2¼	2	2
RPI ex. MIPs	3	2½	2¼	2	2	2
Money GDP	5	6	5½	5	4¾	4¾

[1] *Forecasts for 1995–96 and 1996–97 and assumptions thereafter.*

Output   **3.62**   The rate at which the economy can safely grow over the medium term depends on the current degree of spare capacity (the output gap) and the growth rate of productive potential (trend output), which is determined by the supply-side performance of the economy.

Spare capacity   **3.63**   There is a great deal of uncertainty surrounding estimates both of the current output gap and the trend growth rate. The output gap, which opened up during the 1990–1992 recession, has probably narrowed since 1993 as the economy has on average grown above its trend rate. Nevertheless there probably is still a negative output gap in the economy as a whole. While the CBI survey, for example, shows capacity utilisation at relatively high levels in the manufacturing sector, such measures take little account of the degree of slack in the labour market. There is little evidence of shortages of skilled labour, even in manufacturing. Moreover there is undoubtedly a substantial margin of spare capacity outside the manufacturing sector – for example, in construction. The existence of spare capacity means that the economy should be able to grow at above its trend rate for a time without putting upward pressure on inflation.

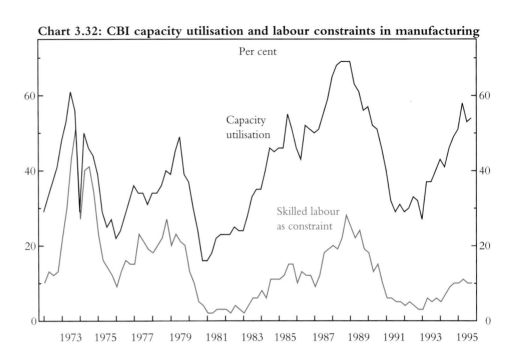

Chart 3.32: CBI capacity utilisation and labour constraints in manufacturing

Supply-side performance

3.64   One way of assessing the growth of productive potential is to disaggregate it into three elements: the growth of productivity; the growth of the labour supply; and changes in the sustainable level of unemployment.

3.65   Quantitatively the most important of these elements is the underlying rate of productivity growth. There was a significant improvement in the UK's overall productivity performance over the 1980s, compared both with that of other countries and with the UK's performance in the 1970s. The pick-up in productivity growth was more marked in manufacturing, where it was sufficient to make good much of the earlier deterioration in the UK's productivity levels relative to its major competitors.

3.66   Supply-side reforms are likely to have made a major contribution to this improved performance. The strengthening of competition and market forces gave firms the incentive to take measures to improve efficiency, and the better climate of industrial relations enabled them to introduce such improvements more easily. Although whole economy productivity growth in the 1980s was not as fast as in the 1950s and 1960s, the latter was a period when most other OECD countries were growing very rapidly, spurred by the liberalisation of trade, reconstruction and the wide productivity gap that had opened up with the US.

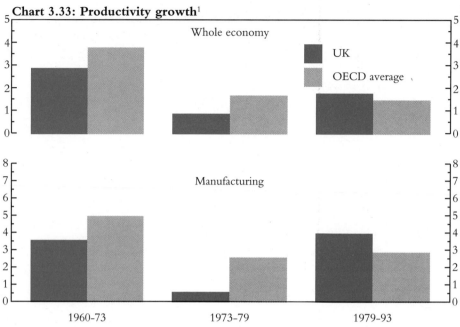

Chart 3.33: Productivity growth[1]

[1] *Per cent. UK figures for whole economy exclude oil.*

3.67   Supply-side performance is also likely to have benefited from greater labour market flexibility. Working patterns are more varied, wage determination has become more decentralised and links between pay and performance are stronger. The cyclical peak in unemployment in the early 1990s was lower than in the previous cycle, and there is evidence that the sustainable rate of unemployment has declined.

3.68   The improvement in productivity growth over the 1980s should be at least sustained over the rest of this decade, as the impact of supply-side reforms continues to be felt. In addition, the labour supply is likely to be boosted by demographic trends, and possibly also by a renewed rise in female participation. The Government's labour market reforms may also boost productive potential by promoting further falls in unemployment.

3.69   Considering these factors together, it is plausible to assume that the trend growth rate is currently around 2½ per cent per annum. This would be broadly in line with the average growth rate achieved over the post-war period as a whole. It is possible that trend growth will be higher than this if the impact of supply-side reforms is greater than allowed for. But in terms of planning the public finances it is sensible to err on the side of caution.

Output projections   **3.70**   The projections for output in Table 3.9 show the economy growing slightly above trend, at 3 per cent in 1997–98 and 2¾ per cent per annum thereafter. This implies that the current margin of spare capacity in the economy is gradually taken up as output returns to its trend level.

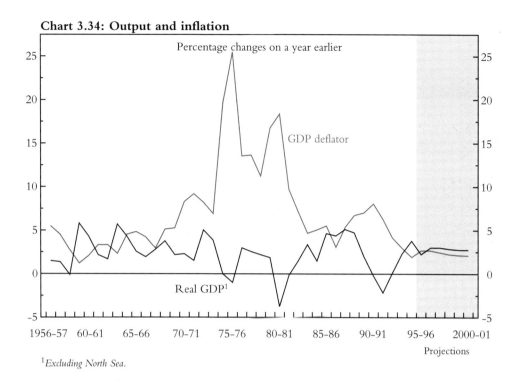

Chart 3.34: Output and inflation

Percentage changes on a year earlier

GDP deflator

Real GDP[1]

1956-57 60-61   65-66   70-71   75-76   80-81   85-86   90-91   95-96   2000-01

Projections

[1]*Excluding North Sea.*

Inflation projections

3.71 With the economy projected to continue operating below capacity over the medium term, the rate of increase in the GDP deflator is assumed to fall gradually after 1996–97, reaching 2 per cent by 1999–2000. RPI excluding MIPs inflation is projected to follow a similar profile but is slightly lower on average (historically there has been a tendency for the GDP deflator to rise slightly faster than the RPI). These inflation projections are consistent with achievement of the Government's target for RPI excluding MIPs inflation of 2½ per cent or less by the end of this Parliament and beyond.

Changes since the last Budget

3.72 Table 3.10 compares the medium-term economic projections with those in the November 1994 Budget. Growth has been slightly lower than expected this year. Inflation – as measured by the increase in the GDP deflator – has also been lower than expected in 1995–96, but is projected to be slightly higher over the medium term. By the end of the period the price level is slightly above that in last year's Budget projections.

Table 3.10   Differences from 1994 Budget projections

	Percentage points				
	1995–96	1996–97	1997–98	1998–99	1999–2000
Real GDP growth					
Non-North Sea	−¾	¼	¼	0	0
Total	−¾	¼	¼	0	0
Inflation					
GDP Deflator	−½	¼	¼	¼	0

Annex A to Chapter 3
Forecasts of GDP and its components

Table 3A.1 Forecasts of gross domestic product and its components

	£ billion at 1990 prices, seasonally adjusted										
	Consumers' expenditure	General government consumption	Total fixed investment	Stock-building	Domestic demand	Exports of goods and services	**Total final expenditure**	*Less* imports of goods and services	*Less* adjustment to factor cost	*Plus* statistical discrepancy[1]	**GDP at factor cost**
1994	358·2	118·3	99·5	2·6	578·6	154·9	733·6	161·9	74·9	−0·5	496·3
1995	366·7	119·1	100·5	3·8	590·1	163·9	754·0	168·0	76·7	0·1	509·3
1996	379·3	119·5	104·9	3·1	606·9	175·8	782·7	179·3	79·5	0·1	524·0
1994 1st half	178·1	59·1	50·1	0·0	287·3	75·6	362·9	79·8	37·2	−0·3	245·6
2nd half	180·1	59·2	49·4	2·6	291·4	79·3	370·7	82·1	37·7	−0·2	250·7
1995 1st half	182·0	59·4	50·4	1·5	293·3	80·7	373·9	82·3	38·1	0·0	253·6
2nd half	184·7	59·7	50·1	2·3	296·9	83·2	380·1	85·8	38·7	0·1	255·7
1996 1st half	188·0	59·6	52·0	1·6	301·2	86·5	387·7	88·6	39·4	0·1	259·8
2nd half	191·4	59·9	53·0	1·5	305·7	89·3	395·0	90·8	40·1	0·0	264·2
1997 1st half	195·1	59·9	53·9	1·2	310·2	92·1	402·2	93·5	40·8	0·1	267·9
	Percentage changes on a year earlier[2]										
1994	2¾	2	3	½	3	9	4¼	5¼	3	0	4
1995	2¼	¾	1	¼	2	5¾	2¾	3¾	2½	0	2¾
1996	3½	¼	4¼	−¼	2¾	7¼	3¾	6¾	3½	0	3
1997 1st half	3¾	½	3¾	−¼	3	6½	3¾	5½	3¾	0	3¼

1 *Expenditure adjustment.*

2 *For stockbuilding and the statistical discrepancy, changes are expressed as a percent of GDP.*

Annex B to Chapter 3
The Panel of Independent Forecasters[1]

Short-term economic outlook

Policy projections **3B.1** Our forecasts use different projections of economic policy[2], which do not necessarily coincide with the policy recommendations we make.

Interest rates **3B.2** Interest rates have not been raised as some of us had expected last May. Forecasts for 1995 are now distinguished between those who expect a ½ percentage point cut at the end of the year and those who expect no change. None of us expects interest rates to increase over the next year or so. Congdon and Minford expect a ½ percentage point cut at the end of this year and Minford expects a further ¾ percentage point cut by the end of next year. Davies expects a small cut next year. Britton and Currie expect no change in interest rates throughout. As usual Godley assumes no change in interest rates.

The Budget **3B.3** Most of us assume that public expenditure in cash terms will be broadly as planned. On top of this we expect tax cuts of £2–5 billion, although tax cuts could be larger to the extent that there are offsetting cuts in expenditure. Minford expects net tax cuts of £4 billion this year and next. Godley assumes full indexation of the tax system, but since this eliminates real fiscal drag it implies modest tax cuts as against a base which is only indexed for inflation.

Sterling **3B.4** At the time of our last meeting there was considerable uncertainty about sterling which had depreciated by 5½ per cent in effective terms between the end of 1994 and May. The sterling ERI fell by a further ¾ per cent to July but has since stabilised. At our last meeting views differed between those who expected sterling to remain flat at its current level and those who expected it to appreciate towards its end-1994 level. Now we all expect sterling to remain around its current level until the end of this year, ie the sterling ERI around 84–86, although Currie and Congdon still expect sterling to appreciate to around 87½ by late 1996.

The world economy **3B.5** There is now plenty of evidence that the growth of the world economy slowed at the start of the year and most of us have shaded down our forecasts for world growth to around 2½ per cent for this year and next. Although world trade growth has also slowed, this is only in relation to the extremely rapid growth last year. Davies estimates that quarter-on-quarter OECD trade growth was still over 9 per cent (at an annual rate) in each of the first two quarters of this year.

---

[1] *This annex reproduces the sections on the short-term and medium-term economic outlook from the report of the Panel of Independent Forecasters submitted to the Chancellor of the Exchequer on 2 November 1995. The full report, which includes members' individual submissions on the economic outlook and policy and a special report on the monetary framework, is available from HM Treasury.*

[2] *To most of us these are unconditional forecasts of Government policy. Godley assumes unchanged fiscal and monetary stance in order to reveal what changes in policy may be necessary.*

3B.6   In the US the slowdown in the first half of this year reflected a stock adjustment. We do not believe the US is heading for a recession; indeed once the stock adjustment is completed the economy may pick up, as shown by the strong growth recorded in the third quarter. One factor which may restrain world growth is the effect of fiscal consolidation in some European economies. This is likely to depress growth, but without causing a recession since lower interest rates may partly offset the more contractionary fiscal stance.

World real interest rates   **3B.7**   A recent G10 study identified that there had been an increase in world real interest rates, after allowing for inflation expectations, of about 100 basis points over the last 35 years, to around 4 per cent. (In the UK context, real interest rates are even higher at present if they are calculated using the GDP deflator rather than the RPI excluding MIPs.) Real interest rates actually rose in the early 1980s, reflecting slow adjustment of inflation expectations after the experience of the 1970s. Inflation expectations, and any premium associated with inflation uncertainty, have probably fallen now, but rising public debt, and to a lesser extent increasing rates of return on private capital, have prevented any fall back in real interest rates. Moreover, on a global scale neither of these factors seems likely to be reversed.

Commodity prices   **3B.8**   The Economist index of commodity prices has fallen back, but other measures of commodity prices are still rising, albeit at a lower rate. Davies believes that non-oil commodity prices have probably already turned back up and will continue to grow at a moderate rate along with growth in the world economy. Oil prices may remain pretty flat, however. Minford, on the other hand, expects commodity prices to fall in response to the slowdown in world growth.

World inflation   **3B.9**   Those of us who have revised down our forecasts for world growth have also revised down our forecasts for inflation a little; all our inflation forecasts are now close to 2½ per cent for 1995 and 1996.

UK overview   **3B.10**   The UK economy has slowed along with the other major economies. During 1994 the economy grew at 4 per cent, while GDP grew by 2½ per cent over the year to the third quarter of 1995. The recovery in the labour market has eased off with claimant unemployment falling less rapidly since May. Inflation has picked up a little, but this largely reflects higher import prices due to the depreciation of sterling at the start of this year and the rise in commodity prices last year, rather than domestic demand pressures. The current account has deteriorated, largely because of a fall back in the surplus on net investment income from the exceptional level last year. The PSBR is likely to exceed the levels forecast in the last Budget.

Table 3B.1   Summary of short-term forecasts

| | | Percentage changes on a year earlier unless otherwise stated | | |
| | | Average | Range | |
			Lowest	Highest
Real GDP	1995	2·7	2·6	2·8
	1996	2·7	2·5	3·1
Unemployment (millions)	1995 Q4	2·3	2·2	2·3
	1996 Q4	2·1	1·8	2·23
RPI excluding MIPs	1995 Q4	2·9	2·6	3·3
	1996 Q4	2·6	1·8	3·3[1]
Current account (£ billion)	1995	−6·0	−8·9	−2·9
	1996	−3·7	−9·4	1·5
PSBR (£ billion)	1995–96	27·4	25·2	30·0
	1996–97	22·0	20·2	26·0

[1] *Derived from forecast of consumer price index.*

Demand and activity

3B.11 We expect GDP to grow by about 2¾ per cent in 1995 and 2½ to 3 per cent in 1996. Although the range of forecasts for growth is narrow in comparison with some of our previous reports, this should be seen in the context of different policy assumptions: for some of us a relaxation of policy is the reason why growth is sustained.

Composition of demand

3B.12 Most of us expect net trade to make a positive contribution to growth this year, ranging from ½ per cent in the case of Godley to 1¼ per cent in the case of Britton. Davies expects a negative contribution of ¼ per cent. In 1996 most of us expect a positive contribution of about ½ per cent, but Congdon expects roughly no contribution and Britton expects a large positive contribution of 1 per cent. The forecasts for domestic demand show a marked slowdown in 1995, to 1½–2¼ per cent, and a modest pick-up in 1996, to 2–2½ per cent, apart from Britton and Davies who expect it to remain around 1½ and 2¼ per cent respectively.

Table 3B.2   Forecasts of domestic demand

| | | Percentage changes on a year earlier | | |
| | | Average | Range | |
			Lowest	Highest
Domestic demand	1995	1·9	1·6	2·3
	1996	2·2	1·6	2·6
Consumer spending	1995	1·9	1·7	2·2
	1996	2·4	2·1	3·0
Fixed investment	1995	2·6	1·6	3·2
	1996	4·6	3·4	6·4
Stockbuilding[1]	1995	0·1	0·0	0·2
	1996	−0·3	−0·6	0·1
Government consumption	1995	0·7	0·25	1·5
	1996	0·9	−0·3	1·7

[1] *Contribution to GDP growth, per cent.*

Consumption   **3B.13**   Our forecasts show consumers' expenditure growth of around 2 per cent this year and 2 to 3 per cent next year. We do not expect much change in the saving ratio, however. In the past the most volatile element of personal savings has been borrowing, which is dominated by mortgage borrowing. The dip in the saving ratio in the late 1980s, which reached a low of 5½ per cent in the middle of 1988, was associated with people realising capital gains on housing. Without a recovery in the housing market, a sharp fall in the saving ratio seems unlikely to most of us. Also the growth of private pensions, job insecurity and high real interest rates may sustain saving at high levels. Davies, while agreeing with the rest of us on the most likely level, thinks that there is a significant risk of a sudden sharp decline in saving if consumer confidence improves as the recovery matures going into 1997.

Investment   **3B.14**   The increase in business investment has been more moderate than most of us had expected. But there is some evidence that investment is picking up at last. Manufacturing investment grew by over 11 per cent in the year to 1995Q2, and other non-oil business investment increased by almost 5 per cent, but oil investment fell.

3B.15   There has been a remarkable contrast between the strength of US and UK investment over the course of the recovery. The US initially started with similar problems to the UK: a surplus of commercial buildings; heavy indebtedness; and asset prices in collapse. But US investment has grown at close to record rates since the trough of the recession, while UK investment has been slow to recover. Share prices have risen sharply in both countries since the end of last year – the FT-SE index is up over 16 per cent on the end of last year – and this should be a stimulus to investment. In the UK, real rates of return are also high and the corporate sector has a very large financial surplus, which could be used to sustain a surge in investment. Britton believes that the large financial surplus is more important for investment by non-manufacturing companies. For manufacturers, it is the attractiveness of the UK as a location for investment that matters, because the surplus could easily be invested in other countries. In fact the UK appears well-placed in this respect as well.

3B.16   One factor which may underlie the relatively weak recovery of UK investment is that capacity utilisation remains low in some sectors, such as construction, although reliable indicators are hard to come by. The BCC survey actually suggests that service utilisation is quite high, but we do not attach much weight to this indicator because the concept of capacity in the service sector is ambiguous and the series has not been available for very long. In manufacturing, the CBI measure of capacity utilisation has fallen recently, although it remains high.

3B.17   Outside the business sector, private housing investment is likely to remain subdued over the next 18 months, while general government investment is being cut back. In these circumstances we expect that manufacturing and oil investment will increase their share of total investment over the next three to four years.

3B.18   Apart from Congdon, we have all revised down our forecasts for investment in 1995. We expect growth of between 1½ to 3¼ per cent this year. Minford, who includes stocks and consumer durables, expects growth of over 5 per cent. In 1996 everyone expects growth to increase; the forecasts range between 3½ and 6½ per cent.

Stockbuilding **3B.19**   We are concerned about the build-up in stocks, which have been high for the last three quarters. Even without destocking, lower stockbuilding would make a negative contribution to growth. For most of us, the pattern of stockbuilding is the main reason for the slowdown in activity in the second half of this year or early next year. Some of us think this might be enough to produce a fall in GDP in the quarter-on-quarter figures, though none of us are actually forecasting this in our central projections. One difficulty in interpreting the data is that a large part of the increase in stockbuilding is due to the CSO's alignment adjustment, which may get revised away as the output and expenditure accounts are reconciled.

3B.20   One puzzle is the build-up of stocks in the retail sector. Some of this may be part of a longer term trend towards retailers holding stocks that were previously held elsewhere in the economy, for instance by wholesalers. Indeed survey evidence of retailers does not indicate that they are holding excessive stocks. Retailers may also be attempting to get things moving in the hope that stocks will attract buyers. But it is also possible that the build-up is partly related to sluggish retail sales and is involuntary.

Trade volumes **3B.21**   Net trade contributed 1¼ per cent to GDP growth in the first quarter of this year, and minus ¾ per cent in the second quarter. In contrast to the experience of last year, the positive contribution was due to surprisingly low import volumes rather than exports which were flat. In the second quarter, exports fell by ¾ per cent while imports recovered.

Exports **3B.22**   The weak export performance in the first half of this year is puzzling. No doubt it is partly related to the slowdown in world trade. But we do not think world trade growth stopped; it just fell back from the extremely rapid growth rates seen last year. This implies that the UK lost market share in the first half of the year. There are plenty of theories about what is going on but it is hard to know how much importance to attach to each of them.

3B.23   Some of us think that there may be a substantial measurement problem, with export prices over-recorded and volumes under-recorded. Relating CBI export orders or prices to the official data supports this view (see Appendix 1 to Congdon's submission on the latter). The difference between the survey and official data has narrowed recently, as the surveys indicate weakening orders, but on the basis of past experience orders are still consistent with growing export volumes.

3B.24   Others think that what has happened is consistent with a view of the UK as a small open economy facing temporary capacity constraints. As part of a small economy, UK exporters take world prices as given in foreign currency terms. This explains why exporters allowed their prices to rise in sterling terms after the 1992 devaluation and again earlier this year. Higher prices raised export profit margins, and when there was still substantial spare capacity firms put in a big marketing effort, and exports grew strongly. Recently capacity constraints have started to bite, as demonstrated by the increase in the proportion of firms reporting delivery dates as a constraint, and exports have slowed.

3B.25   Others think that this year's weak export growth is explained by the effect of the 1992 devaluation wearing off. The data on export price competitiveness indicate that the boost to price competitiveness was very short-lived. But the proportion of firms who regard prices as a constraint on exports has increased steadily since the start of 1993, indicating that this effect may have been quite long drawn out. In any case, much of the improvement in cost competitiveness has been maintained, but the lack of further recent improvement could explain some of the slowdown in export growth.

3B.26 Those of us who think that there is a measurement problem are optimistic about export prospects. Those who think that exporters are capacity constrained are also optimistic, at least in the longer term, because with exports so profitable, firms should be willing to install extra capacity which will boost exports. The evidence on manufacturing investment suggests that this process has already started. Some of us think that the tradeable sector is in such a strong position that there will be growth in net trade even without a recovery in world trade. The pessimists focus on the effect of the devaluation wearing off and the possible lack of price competitiveness. Provided the required level of investment materialises Godley sees no cause for concern. But, on the evidence to date, he fears there will be inadequate investment.

3B.27 Our forecasts for exports of goods and services is for growth of between 4¾ and 6½ per cent in 1995 and 4¾ to 7½ per cent in 1996. One factor strengthening the UK's position is that North Sea oil production is likely to reach a new peak in the next year or so.

Imports **3B.28** Some of us think that the recent figures on imports are also suspect. Britton thinks that the weakness of import volumes is particularly odd given the structure of demand, with growth in investment and stocks so important. However, others argue that the increase in import prices this year can be explained satisfactorily by the depreciation and higher commodity prices, which may have a lagged effect because of the widespread use of forward contracts. Minford thinks that the weakness of imports can be explained by the profitability of import substitution activities, especially given the improvements in quality. Our forecasts for import growth in 1995 are between 1¼ and 3½ per cent, and 3¾ and 4½ per cent for 1996.

Table 3B.3   Forecasts of net trade and the current account

		Average	Range	
			Lowest	Highest
Export volumes[1]	1995	5·5	4·7	6·5
(per cent growth)	1996	5·6	4·8[3]	7·4
Import volumes[1]	1995	2·5	1·2	3·5[3]
(per cent growth)	1996	4·1	3·8	4·6
Net trade[2]	1995	0·7	−0·3	1·2
	1996	0·4	0·1	0·9
Current account	1995	−6·0	−8·9	−2·9
(£ billion)	1996	−3·7	−9·4	1·5

[1] Goods and services.
[2] Contribution to GDP growth, per cent.
[3] Non-oil.

Current account **3B.29** The current account has deteriorated since the end of last year. In the second half of 1994 the current account was in balance, but in the first half of 1995 there was a deficit of £3¾ billion. Net investment income accounts for £3 billion of this deterioration and the balance on transfers contributes another £¾ billion, while the balance on goods and services has hardly changed.

3B.30 Some fall back in net investment income was widely anticipated because last year's performance was affected by special factors, such as exceptional losses made by foreign banks operating in the UK. The figures for 1995 already show an improvement in the performance of UK-based foreign banks which makes the UK's current account worse. There have also been some exceptional items adding to the deterioration in net investment income this year, such as losses arising from the collapse of Barings.

3B.31 On average our forecasts of the current account deficit for 1995 have increased since last May. This is partly because we had expected stronger export growth. Next year, apart from Godley, we all expect the deficit to narrow, and Minford and Congdon forecast a small surplus.

Labour market **3B.32** The recovery in the labour market appears to be losing momentum. Employment growth has slowed, and the rate of decline of unemployment has slowed sharply. Earnings growth appears to have fallen slightly.

3B.33 Revisions to the employer-based measure of **employment** appeared to reconcile it with the household based LFS. But there remained wide differences in the male/female and full-time/part-time composition of employment changes, which suggested that the similar trends in overall employment only provided a superficial reconciliation. In the latest data, the two aggregate measures have moved apart again. The reasons for these discrepancies are not clear. However, if we look at other evidence, such as the behaviour of unemployment, and the implied patterns of male and female participation, the LFS figures appear to give a more coherent account of labour market behaviour.

3B.34 According to the summer LFS the number of GB employees plus self-employed has increased by 650,000 since the trough in winter 1992–93. But employment is still over 680,000 less than the previous peak in spring 1990. On a full-time equivalent basis, where part-timers count as a half, employment has increased by about 465,000 since the trough, reflecting the increasing importance of female employment growth, much of it part time (nevertheless according to the LFS, male employment has also risen some 200,000 from its trough in 1993). Employment in terms of full-time equivalents is still over a million less than its previous peak. The LFS measure of unemployment has fallen by about ½ million since its peak in winter 1992–93 but is still over ½ million above its previous low in spring 1990. The population of working age has increased throughout the period; 360,000 higher by winter 1992–93, and a further 165,000 higher by summer 1995. Putting these numbers together it is clear that there has been a substantial increase in the numbers counted as economically inactive, and participation rates have fallen. Using the figures for total jobs, the fall in participation occurred between 1990 and 1992–93, as we would expect over the course of a typical cycle, but the peculiar feature of the recovery since then is that participation has not picked up. If we allow for the growth of part-time employment in the recovery, the participation rate has continued to fall over 1992–93 to 1995.

3B.35 The latest LFS data show that employment increased by over 120,000 between April and July, while the employers' measure increased by just 34,000 between March and June. Our forecasts for employment growth in 1995 range from ½ to 1 per cent. Apart from Britton, who expects a slight fall, everyone expects employment growth of around ¾ per cent in 1996.

3B.36   The UK claimant count measure of **unemployment** is now over 710,000 below its end-1992 peak. But the rate of decline has slowed, averaging only around 12,000 a month from May to September, compared with almost 25,000 a month at the start of the year and almost 50,000 a month in the last three months of 1994. The LFS measure of GB unemployment showed a small rise of 28,000 between the winter and spring quarters, but fell by 18,000 between the spring and summer quarters.

3B.37   In line with these developments we expect claimant count unemployment to be broadly flat at around 2¼ million for the rest of this year. In 1996 Minford expects a fall in unemployment of 0·4 million and the continued growth of part-time employment. The rest of us expect a fall of ¼ million or less. This difference is only partly explained by Minford's forecast of faster output growth. Most of us are assuming that the combination of the introduction of the jobseeker's allowance, which will reduce unemployment, and the tightening of medical conditions for incapacity benefit, which will increase unemployment, will be broadly offsetting. The initial evidence is that the new medical tests are not taking as many people off incapacity benefit as DSS had originally suggested.

3B.38   A key issue is the extent to which **participation** will rise in future; to the extent that it does, less of any given increase in employment will be reflected in a fall in unemployment. Most of the increase in employment in the summer LFS came from greater participation rather than less unemployment. But given that the fall in participation is related to increases in the numbers receiving invalidity benefits and more early retirement, some of the reduction in participation is likely to persist. Another factor has been the increase in participation in higher and further education, part of which is clearly a trend and part of which might be a cyclical effect.

Inflation   **3B.39**   The increase in inflation this year largely reflects the gradual pass through of higher import prices to retail prices. Our forecasts for underlying inflation for the end of this year are all around 3 to 3¼ per cent, apart from Britton and Minford who expect inflation of 2½ and 2¾ per cent respectively. For the end of next year our forecasts range from 1¾ per cent to 3¼ per cent. All the forecasts are within the Government's 1–4 per cent target range, but only Minford and Congdon anticipate inflation below 2½ per cent at the end of next year. Since May most of us have revised down our forecasts for 1996, but the range of our forecasts has not narrowed.

3B.40   If the £50 electricity rebate associated with the flotation of the National Grid is treated as a price reduction, it would have the effect of temporarily reducing the RPI early next year. Inflation would be around 1¼ per cent lower than it otherwise would have been next March and April, but 1¼ per cent higher in March and April 1997. The key point is that this is just a temporary change in the price level and should not affect the conduct of policy. In other words, the effect of the rebates should be excluded when judging the behaviour of the RPI excluding mortgage interest payments against the Government's target.

3B.41 As in previous reports Congdon and Minford are the most optimistic about inflation. They believe that there is still plenty of spare capacity in the economy as a whole. This is reflected in their estimates of the **output gap.** Congdon thinks that the output gap is around the OECD's latest estimate of 2 to 2½ per cent, while Minford thinks it is much larger, possibly more than 6 per cent. They emphasise the degree of slack in the labour market, which they regard as the only constraint in the long run because firms can always install more physical capacity. They believe that there is plenty of slack in the labour market, unemployment is high and the CBI survey shows that even manufacturing firms are not reporting serious skill shortages. Minford is the most optimistic and thinks that unemployment may understate the degree of slack in the labour market. This is partly because he thinks that participation could increase substantially, for instance employment on a full-time equivalent basis is still a million below what it was in 1990. The rest of us think that, while some part-timers may want full-time jobs, this should not be overstated as the trend towards greater part-time employment has been going on for a long time. Minford also thinks that trend productivity growth in the service sector has improved markedly. The rest of us think that the expansion of high productivity service sector jobs is likely to be offset by more low productivity services.

3B.42 To differing degrees, Britton, Currie, Davies and Godley think that the economy's potential to grow has been reduced since the recession by low investment and a small demographic increase in the underlying labour force. Consequently they do not think that the output gap is currently very large. Moreover, some of us think that the output gap is not a very useful concept at present because different sectors have different degrees of capacity utilisation. Also, while we recognise that unemployment remains high, we do not think that a large number of the unemployed can be absorbed back into employment without inflation increasing unless active labour market measures are pursued. Other indicators, such as vacancies and the proportion of people not working, suggest the labour market has tightened.

Table 3B.4 Inflation forecasts

| | | Percentage changes on a year earlier | | |
| | | Average | Range | |
			Lowest	Highest
RPI excluding MIPs	1995 Q4	2·9	2·6	3·3
	1996 Q4	2·6	1·8	3·3[1]
RPI	1995 Q4	3·4	3·0	3·7
	1996 Q4	2·5	1·5	3·5
Average earnings	1995	3·5	3·0[2]	3·7
	1996	4·3	3·9	4·8

[1] *Derived from forecast of consumer price index.*
[2] *Average earnings.*

3B.43 So far this year, **earnings** growth has remained subdued and generally we have revised down our forecasts since May. The underlying rate of increase in average earnings for the economy as a whole was 3¼ per cent in July and August, which brings earnings growth back to the levels seen in 1993. Earnings are growing more rapidly in manufacturing than in services. Godley fears that the growth in manufacturing pay may spread to other sectors. Our forecasts range from 3–3¾ per cent in 1995 and 4–4¾ per cent in 1996.

3B.44   Those of us who are relatively pessimistic about the outlook for earnings point to the pick-up in settlements. The pick-up in settlements combined with the fall in earnings implies that the difference, wage drift, has been squeezed. Davies thinks that drift could easily rebound. However, Minford thinks that, since settlements largely relate to the unionised sector, the squeeze on drift may just reflect the workings of market forces on earnings which may feed through to settlements in time.

3B.45   One aspect of the recent subdued growth in earnings is that labour's share of income is low relative to that of profits. Most of us think this is a purely cyclical effect, especially when one takes account of self-employment income, and we expect the labour share to recover as the output gap closes. On the other hand high real interest rates mean the profit share has to be higher.

Monetary aggregates   **3B.46**   The 12-month growth of **M0**, 5¼ per cent in October, has slowed since late last year, but remains well in excess of the Government's 0–4 per cent medium-term monitoring range. Special factors (such as the National Lottery, high tourist expenditure and cross-Channel shopping) may have played a part, but the underlying reason for continuing rapid M0 growth may be slower velocity growth in a low inflation environment.

3B.47   **M4** has been steadily accelerating since the end of last year. The 12-month growth rate rose from 4¾ per cent last August and 6 per cent in May to 8¼ per cent in September. Underfunding of the PSBR has contributed to this acceleration, although this may unwind over the course of the year. There has also been a pick-up in M4 lending, especially to the corporate sector, and because of more non-mortgage borrowing by the personal sector. Some of the increase in corporate borrowing is being used to finance take-overs, rather than to support organic expansion. But with inflation low, there has been a marked increase in real money growth. Congdon, who attaches great importance to broad money growth, is not particularly concerned about the recent increase and expects it to boost activity next year, leading to a resumption of trend or above-trend growth in 1996. Only if broad money were still growing at high rates in 1997 and 1998, when the output gap may have closed, would he become concerned about the need for policy tightening.

PSBR   **3B.48**   Forecasts of the **PSBR** for 1995–96 range from £25–30 billion, with Currie at the lower end and Britton at the upper end. The forecasts are all well above last year's Budget forecast of £21½ billion. The deterioration largely reflects a shortfall in tax receipts. Davies estimates that, compared with last year's Budget, around two-thirds of the shortfall can be explained by lower inflation and lower real GDP, leaving one-third to be explained by a decline in effective tax rates. Everyone expects some fall in the PSBR next year, even allowing for tax cuts, and the forecasts range from £20¼–26 billion. Godley believes the PSBR is a misleading indicator of the government's financial position because of the effect of asset sales. He concentrates on the general government financial deficit gross of sales of existing houses, which he expects to be £41 billion in 1995 and £38 billion in 1996.

Medium-term prospects

3B.49   This section presents our views on the outlook for the medium term. Our projections are summarised in Table 3B.6.

3B.50   Most of us estimate that trend **growth** is around 2 to 2½ per cent per annum, though Minford would put it rather higher at around 3 per cent. Britton, Davies and Godley project growth at around trend; Congdon, Currie and Minford project growth at slightly above trend. Given Minford's higher estimate of trend, he projects actual growth in the medium term at around 3½ per cent.

3B.51   Everyone projects further reductions in **unemployment**. The degree to which unemployment falls corresponds to the projections for output growth. Godley has a fall of 100,000 next year and then forecasts it to remain flat at 2·1 million. Davies and Britton project falls of around 100,000 per year from 1996 on. Congdon and Currie show larger falls of about 200,000 per year in 1996 and 1997, with a further fall of about 100,000 in 1998 (Currie only). Minford has the largest falls, 300,000 in 1996, 500,000 in 1997 and 400,000 in 1998. By 1998 the forecasts of unemployment range from 1·1 to 2 million. This partly reflects the degree of uncertainty surrounding estimates of the economy's NAIRU or natural rate.

3B.52   Our views on the size of the current output gap are given in paragraphs 42 and 43 and these affect our medium-term **inflation** projections. Minford and Congdon project RPI ex MIPs inflation to be below 2½ per cent. Currie and Britton project inflation around 2½ to 2¾ per cent, with Currie having slightly more inflation and growth. Davies and Godley, who are at the lower end of the range of views on output growth, are at the upper-end of the range of forecasts on inflation, at around 3½ per cent.

3B.53   None of us projects substantial **current account** imbalances in the medium term. Godley has the largest imbalance with a deficit of about 1¾ per cent of GDP by 1998. He warns that there could be a much larger current account deficit if demand grew significantly above the growth of productive potential.

3B.54   All the forecasts for the **PSBR** show it continuing to fall to 1998–99. But the range of projections for 1998–99 is wide, from £17¾ billion to just over £6 billion. As one might expect, with the fastest output growth and largest fall in unemployment, Minford's projection is the lowest. Godley, who forecasts the general government financial deficit gross of sales of existing houses, believes fiscal prospects are much worse because of the prospective rise in interest rates and projects a financial deficit gross of sales of around £34 billion in 1998.

Table 3B.5   Summary of Panel members' short-term forecasts

| | | Percentage changes on a year earlier unless otherwise stated | | | | | | |
		Britton	Congdon	Currie	Davies	Godley	Minford	Average
GDP	1994	3·9	3·9	3·9	3·9	3·9	3·9	3·9
	1995	2·8	2·8	2·7	2·7	2·6	2·8	2·7
	1996	2·5	2·5	3·1	2·5	2·5	2·9	2·7
Domestic demand	1994	3·3	3·3	3·3	3·3	3·3	3·3	3·3
	1995	1·6	1·8	1·8	2·3	1·8	1·9	1·9
	1996	1·6	2·4	2·6	2·3	2·1	2·3	2·2
Net trade[1]	1994	0·5	0·5	0·5	0·5	0·5	0·5	0·5
	1995	1·2	1·0	0·8	−0·3	0·6	0·9	0·7
	1996	0·9	0·1	0·4	0·2	0·3	0·6	0·4
Unemployment	1994 Q4	2·5	2·5	2·5	2·5	2·5	2·5	2·5
(millions)	1995 Q4	2·3	2·3	2·25	2·28	2·2	2·2	2·3
	1996 Q4	2·2	2·1	2·0	2·23	2·1	1·8	2·1
RPI	1994 Q4	2·6	2·6	2·6	2·6	2·6	2·6	2·6
	1995 Q4	3·1	3·0	3·6	3·6	–	3·7	3·4
	1996 Q4	2·5	1·7	3·1	3·5	–	1·5	2·5
RPI excluding MIPs	1994 Q4	2·3	2·3	2·3	2·3	2·3[2]	2·3	2·3
	1995 Q4	2·6	2·9	3·0	3·3	3·1[2]	2·7	2·9
	1996 Q4	2·6	1·8	3·0	3·0	3·3[2]	1·9	2·6
Short-term interest rates	1994 Q4	6·1	6·1	6·1	6·1	6·1	6·1	6·1
(per cent)	1995 Q4	6·75	6·5	6·75	6·8	6·75	6·6	6·7
	1996 Q4	6·75	6·25	6·75	6·5	6·75	5·4	6·4
Current account	1994	−1·7	−1·7	−1·7	−1·7	−1·7	−1·7	−1·7
(£ billion)	1995	−8·2	−2·9	−5·5	−7·5	−8·9	−3·2	−6·0
	1996	−6·5	1·5	−3·2	−4·8	−9·4	0·2	−3·7
PSBR	1994–95	35·9	35·9	35·9	35·9	48·2[3]	35·9	35·9
(£ billion)	1995–96	30·0	28·5	25·2	26·6	41·0[3]	26·6	27·4
	1996–97	26·0	22·0	20·4	20·2	38·0[3]	21·5	22·0

1 *Contribution to GDP growth, per cent.*
2 *Consumer price index.*
3 *General government financial deficit adjusted for net sales of existing assets.*

Table 3B.6   Summary of Panel members' medium-term forecasts

| | | Percentage changes on a year earlier unless otherwise stated | | | | | | |
		Britton	Currie	Davies	Godley	Congdon	Minford	Average
GDP	1995	2·8	2·7	2·7	2·6	2·8	2·8	2·7
	1996	2·5	3·1	2·5	2·5	2·5	2·9	2·7
	1997	2·6	2·8	2·8	2·5	3·1	3·4	2·9
	1998	2·7	2·8	2·5	2·5	–	3·5	2·8
Unemployment	1995	2·31	2·32	2·31	2·2	2·32	2·30	2·3
(millions)	1996	2·18	2·10	2·27	2·1	2·11	1·99	2·1
	1997	2·08	1·93	2·13	2·1	1·89	1·48	1·9
	1998	2·02	1·84	2·04	2·1	–	1·11	1·8
RPI excluding MIPs	1995	2·8	2·9	2·9	3·1[2]	2·8	2·7	2·9
	1996	2·4	3·1	3·1	3·3[2]	1·7	2·1	2·6
	1997	2·6	2·8	3·2	3·6[2]	2·0	2·2	2·7
	1998	2·7	2·5	3·2	3·5[2]	–	2·2	2·8
Current account[1]	1995	−1·2	−0·8	−1·1	−1·5	−0·5	−0·5	−0·9
	1996	−0·9	−0·4	−0·6	−1·5	0·3	0·0	−0·5
	1997	−0·6	−0·6	−0·8	−1·4	−0·5	0·1	−0·6
	1998	−0·3	−0·5	−1·1	−1·7	–	0·0	−0·7
PSBR[1]	1995–96	4·2	3·6	3·7	6·8[3]	4·0	3·7	3·8
	1996–97	3·5	2·7	2·8	6·0[3]	2·9	2·8	2·9
	1997–98	2·7	2·1	1·8	5·3[3]	2·3	2·2	2·2
	1998–99	2·1	1·6	1·1	4·2[3]	–	0·7	1·4

1 *Per cent of GDP.*
2 *Consumer price index.*
3 *General government financial deficit adjusted for net sales of existing assets.*

4　The public finances

Summary

4.01　This chapter sets out projections for the public finances up to 2000–01 after allowing for the measures in the Budget and the new assessment of economic prospects. It also includes an analysis of changes from the 1994 Budget projections. Historical series and further detail on the forecasts for 1995–96 and 1996–97 are presented in Annex A. Annex B provides a guide to the different accounting conventions used in presentation of the public finances in this chapter and elsewhere.

4.02　The public sector borrowing requirement (PSBR) is projected to decrease steadily over the next five years, with budget balance achieved by 1999–2000. This is a year later than projected in last year's Budget, largely as a consequence of lower revenues and thus a higher PSBR for 1995–96 than previously forecast.

The budget deficit

4.03　The projected path for the PSBR is summarised in Table 4.1.

Table 4.1　Public sector borrowing requirement[1]

	Outturn	Forecast		Projection[2]			
	1994–95	1995–96	1996–97	1997–98	1998–99	1999–00	2000–01
£ billion							
General government expenditure	287·8	302·1	308·3	319	329	338	346
General government receipts	250·0	271·9	284·8	304	323	340	359
General government borrowing requirement	37·8	30·2	23·5	16	6	−2	−13
PCMOB[3]	−1·9	−1·2	−1·1	−1	0	0	0
PSBR	**35·9**	**29·0**	**22·4**	**15**	**5**	**−2**	**−14**
Per cent of money GDP							
General government expenditure	42½	42½	41	40¼	39¼	38½	37¾
General government receipts	37	38¼	37¾	38¼	38½	38¾	39
General government borrowing requirement	5½	4¼	3	2	¾	−¼	−1½
PCMOB[3]	−¼	−¼	−¼	0	0	0	0
PSBR	**5¼**	**4**	**3**	**2**	**¾**	**−¼**	**−1½**
Money GDP − £ billion	678	712	754	795	836	876	918

[1] *In this and other tables, constituent items may not sum to totals because of rounding.*
[2] *Projections are rounded to the nearest £1 billion from 1997–98 onwards.*
[3] *Public corporations' market and overseas borrowing.*

The PSBR in the short term

4.04   The outturn for the PSBR in 1994–95 was £35·9 billion, 5¼ per cent of GDP. This represents a fall of £9½ billion from the cyclical peak in borrowing the previous year. The latest forecast for the PSBR in 1995–96 is £29 billion, 4 per cent of GDP, and a further fall of £7 billion on the previous year.

4.05   Taking into account the tax changes announced in the Budget and the new public expenditure plans, the PSBR in 1996–97 is forecast to fall to £22½ billion, 3 per cent of GDP.

4.06   The main driving force behind the fall in the PSBR in 1996–97 is slow growth in public expenditure, reflecting the tight spending plans announced in the Budget. With the Budget tax measures, growth in receipts is expected to be a little below that of money GDP.

Medium-term PSBR projections

4.07   The projections of the public finances in the medium term are based on the assumptions on the economy set out in paragraph 3.61 of Chapter 3. The PSBR is projected to fall steadily, with a small debt repayment projected for 1999–2000 and a larger debt repayment for 2000–01. The main influence is tight control of public expenditure which is projected to fall sharply as a proportion of GDP, in line with the new spending plans. Growth in receipts over the medium term is a little faster than that of GDP, the normal expectation given growth at or above trend and unchanged tax policies (defined as including existing commitments to real increases in road fuel and tobacco duties).

Other measures of the fiscal stance

4.08   Table 4.2 gives an alternative presentation of the fiscal outlook on a national accounts basis (see Annex B). The table sets out projections of the current balance of the public sector and of the financial deficit for both general government and the public sector as a whole, and shows how they relate to the PSBR. The balance on the public sector's current account is forecast to move from a deficit of £19 billion in 1995–96 to a small surplus in 1998–99, with larger surpluses thereafter.

4.09   Net capital spending – the public sector's balance on capital account – is forecast at £12 billion in 1995–96, but is projected to decline to £8 billion in 1998–99, reflecting the reductions in public sector capital spending and the increasing emphasis on private finance in the new spending plans. (Capital expenditure under the Private Finance Initiative is expected to amount to over £7 billion over the three years to 1998–99. This does not score as public sector capital spending.) The public sector financial deficit (PSFD) is projected to fall steadily from £31½ billion in 1995–96 and move into surplus in 1999–2000. The gap between the PSFD and the PSBR closes, and then reverses sign, as privatisation proceeds decline.

4.10   The general government financial deficit (GGFD) – which is also the measure used to monitor budget deficits under the European Union excessive deficits procedure – is forecast at £33½ billion for 1995–96, 4¾ per cent of GDP. By 1996–97, it is forecast to be close to the 3 per cent reference level for deficits used in the excessive deficits procedure, and is projected to fall substantially below that level in subsequent years.

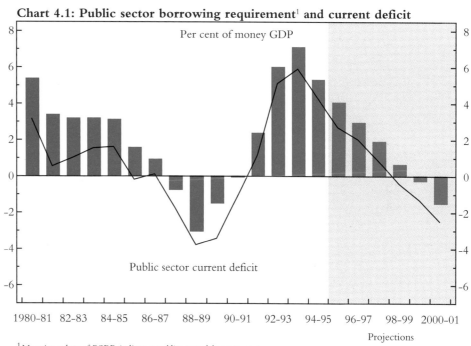

Chart 4.1: Public sector borrowing requirement[1] and current deficit

[1] Negative values of PSBR indicate a public sector debt repayment.

Table 4.2   The public sector's finances

| | Outturn | Forecast | | Projection[4] | | | |
	1994–95	1995–96	1996–97	1997–98	1998–99	1999–00	2000–01
				£ billion			
Receipts[1]	253·9	276·1	289·9	308	327	344	363
Current expenditure[1, 2]	283·3	295·3	305·5	315	324	333	341
Current balance[1]	**−29·4**	**−19·2**	**−15·5**	**−7**	**3**	**11**	**23**
Net capital spending[1, 3, 5]	11·1	12·2	9·9	9	8	8	8
Financial deficit[1]	**40·5**	**31·4**	**25·4**	**16**	**5**	**−3**	**−15**
Privatisation proceeds and other financial transactions	4·6	2·4	3·0	1	0	−1	−1
PSBR	**35·9**	**29·0**	**22·4**	**15**	**5**	**−2**	**−14**
General government financial deficit[1] – £ billion	41·9	33·4	26·1	17	6	−3	−14
– per cent of GDP	6¼	4¾	3½	2	¾	−¼	−1½

[1] Figures on a national accounts basis. See Annex B.
[2] Includes depreciation of fixed capital.
[3] Net of depreciation and less capital transfer receipts.
[4] Rounded to the nearest £1 billion.
[5] Does not include capital expenditure under the Private Finance Initiative, which is expected to amount to £7·2 billion over three years to 1998–99. See Table 6.5.

Public sector debt

4.11   Table 4.3 sets out projections for the stock of net public sector debt and gross general government debt. (Definitions are set out in Annex B.) Net public sector debt at end-March 1995 stood at £291 billion, 41¾ per cent of GDP. The latest forecasts for the PSBR imply a further increase in the ratio in the short term, to a peak of 44½ per cent at end-March 1997. Thereafter the ratio is projected to stabilise and then fall, as the PSBR is brought down further.

Table 4.3   Public sector debt[1]

	Outturn	Forecast		Projection			
	1994–95	1995–96	1996–97	1997–98	1998–99	1999–00	2000–01
Net public sector debt							
£ billion[2]	291	322	344	361	367	366	354
per cent of GDP[3]	41¾	44	44½	44¼	43	40¾	37¾
Gross general government debt							
£ billion[2]	343	378	401	419	426	426	414
per cent of GDP[3]	49¼	51½	51¾	51¼	49¾	47½	44

[1] At end-March.
[2] Rounded to the nearest £1 billion.
[3] GDP centred on end-March. Ratios for excessive deficits procedure use GDP for year ending in March, which raises ratio by around 1¼ to 1½ per cent.

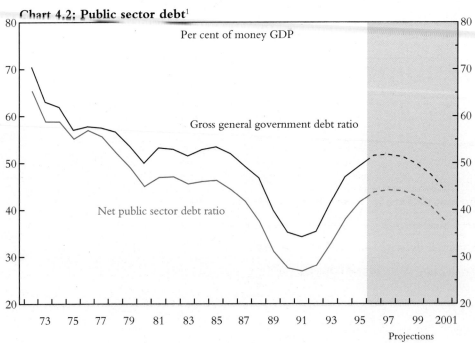

Chart 4.2: Public sector debt[1]

Per cent of money GDP

Gross general government debt ratio

Net public sector debt ratio

Projections

[1]At end-March as a per cent of money GDP in four quarters centred on end-March (see footnote 3 to Table 4.3).

4.12   Gross general government debt, the measure used for the European Union excessive deficits procedure, stood at 49¼ per cent of GDP at end-March 1995. It is projected to rise to 51¾ per cent of GDP at end-March 1997, and to fall back thereafter. The ratio actually used in the excessive deficits procedure uses a slightly different measure of GDP as the denominator; at end-March 1997 the debt/GDP ratio on this basis is projected to be 53¼ per cent, which is comfortably below the 60 per cent reference level.

General government receipts

4.13   Table 4.4 shows the outturns for 1994–95, short-term forecasts for 1995–96 and 1996–97 and medium-term projections up to 2000–01 for general government receipts and its principal components. A more detailed breakdown for the 1994–95 outturns and for the short-term forecasts is shown in Table 4A.1.

Table 4.4   General government receipts

				£ billion			
	Outturn	Forecast		Projection[3]			
	1994–95	1995–96	1996–97	1997–98	1998–99	1999–00	2000–01
Income tax	63·1	68·9	70·2	75	81	86	91
Corporation tax	19·4	24·7	26·6	30	32	34	35
Value added tax	41·8	44·0	47·9	50	53	56	59
Excise duties[1]	27·0	28·3	30·8	33	36	39	42
Other taxes and royalties[2]	40·3	43·8	46·3	49	51	53	57
Social security contributions	42·1	44·4	46·9	49	51	54	56
Other receipts	16·4	17·7	16·1	17	18	18	18
General government receipts	**250·0**	**271·9**	**284·8**	**304**	**323**	**340**	**359**
GGR/GDP ratio – per cent	37	38¼	37¾	38¼	38½	38¾	39

[1] *Fuel, alcohol and tobacco duties.*
[2] *Includes council tax as well as other central government taxes.*
[3] *Rounded to the nearest £1 billion.*

Receipts in 1995–96   **4.14**   General government receipts are now expected to rise by 9 per cent in 1995–96, nearly twice the forecast increase in money GDP. This will be the second year running that growth in general government receipts has been substantially in excess of that of GDP. Much of the rise in receipts relative to GDP reflects the effects of the tax increases in the two 1993 Budgets.

Receipts in 1996–97 and beyond   **4.15**   General government receipts are forecast to rise by 4¾ per cent in 1996–97, a bit slower than the forecast rise in money GDP. The tax changes in this Budget will reduce receipts by £3¼ billion next year (see Tables 1.5 and 5.1), more than offsetting the underlying tendency of receipts to rise relative to GDP as a result of real fiscal drag.

4.16   Thereafter, when the effects of this Budget are largely worked through, receipts are expected to return to their underlying trend of growing slightly faster than GDP. The medium-term receipts projections have been made on the conventional assumption of no further changes in tax rates and an indexed tax system (except for the commitment to real increases for tobacco and road fuel duties).

Taxes as a share of GDP   **4.17**   Following the 1993 tax increases, tax and social security revenues have risen quite sharply as a share of GDP from what was a 20 year low in 1993–94. The tax/GDP ratio is now forecast at 36 per cent in 1995–96, a rise of 2 percentage points on two years earlier.

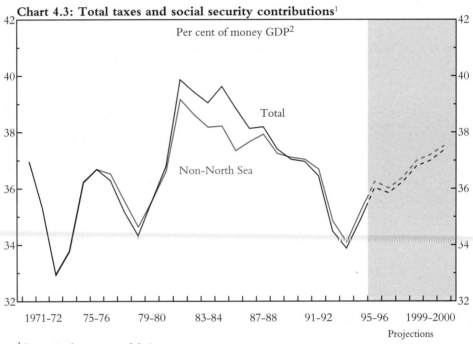

Chart 4.3: Total taxes and social security contributions[1]

[1] On a national accounts accruals basis.
[2] Non-North Sea taxes and social security contributions are expressed as a percent of non-North Sea money GDP.

4.18   A small fall in the tax/GDP ratio is forecast for 1996–97, as a result of the tax reductions announced in this year's Budget. Thereafter, on the conventional assumption of no policy change on taxes, the ratio is projected to rise.

General government expenditure

4.19   The Government's objective for public spending is to reduce it as a share of GDP over time, and in particular to reduce it to below 40 per cent of GDP. On present plans, this objective will be achieved in 1997–98. The objective is expressed in terms of GGE(X), an aggregate which excludes, from total general government expenditure, privatisation proceeds and spending financed out of National Lottery proceeds, and which also nets off interest and dividend receipts from gross payments.

4.20   Table 4.5 shows the 1994–95 outturn, forecasts for 1995–96 and 1996–97 and projections up to 2000–01 for general government expenditure (GGE) and its main components. The projections up to 1998–99 are consistent with the new public spending plans. Figures for later years assume that Control Total spending will grow by ¾ per cent a year in real terms.

Table 4.5   General government expenditure

	Outturn	Forecast		Projection[1]			
	1994–95	1995–96	1996–97	1997–98	1998–99	1999–00	2000–01
Control Total	248·2	255·5	260·2	268	276	283	291
Cyclical social security[2]	14·4	14·0	13·9	14	15	15	16
Central government debt interest	17·6	20·5	22·3	24	24	24	23
Accounting adjustments	9·0	9·6	9·7	9	10	10	11
GGE(X)[3]	**289·2**	**299·6**	**306·1**	**315**	**324**	**332**	**341**
Privatisation proceeds	−6·4	−3·0	−4·0	−2½	−1½	−1	−1
Other adjustments	5·0	5·5	6·2	6	6	6	6
GGE	**287·8**	**302·1**	**308·3**	**319**	**329**	**338**	**346**
GGE(X)[3]/GDP ratio – per cent	42¾	42	40½	39¾	38¾	38	37
Real growth – per cent:							
Control Total	1¼	¼	−1	½	½	¾	¾
GGE(X)[2]	2¼	¾	−½	½	½	½	½

(£ billion)

[1] *Rounded to the nearest £1 billion, except for privatisation proceeds, rounded to nearest £½ billion.*

[2] *Projections assume constant unemployment – see economic assumptions for public expenditure, paragraph 6A.5.*

[3] *Excluding privatisation proceeds and lottery financed spending and net of interest and dividend receipts.*

Expenditure in 1995–96   **4.21**   GGE(X) in 1995–96 is forecast to rise by 3½ per cent, somewhat lower than the expected growth in money GDP. Control Total spending is forecast at £255½ billion, an underspend of £¾ billion on the plans in last year's Budget. In real terms, this represents an increase of ¼ per cent on 1994–95 spending.

Expenditure over the medium term   **4.22**   The new public spending plans provide for Control Total spending to rise at an average of only 2½ per cent a year in cash terms over the next three years. Measured in real terms, this represents a standstill in spending, with the level of real spending projected for 1998–99 much the same as in 1995–96. The projected increase in GGE(X) is only marginally higher and represents average growth in real terms spending over this period of ¼ per cent per annum.

4.23   Outside the Control Total, cyclical social security is projected to increase by only 5 per cent in total over the three years to 1998–99, a real terms fall. Debt interest payments (net of receipts) are projected to continue rising up to 1997–98, but thereafter to flatten off as the level of new borrowing is reduced.

Expenditure as a share of GDP

4.24   The ratio of GGE(X) to GDP fell in 1994–95, from a cyclical peak of 43½ per cent in 1992–93, and is expected to fall further in 1995–96. The new public expenditure plans imply a sharp fall of over 3 percentage points in this ratio over the next three years, falling below 40 per cent from 1997–98 onwards. The medium-term projections show this trend continuing, with the GGE(X)/GDP ratio in 2000–01 down to 37 per cent.

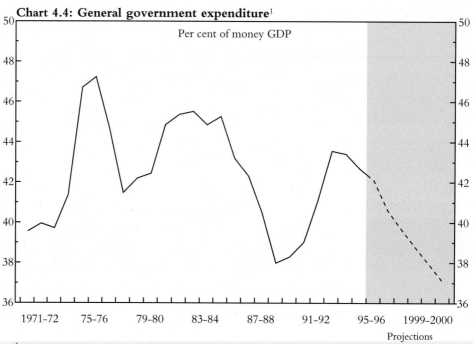

Chart 4.4: General government expenditure[1]

Per cent of money GDP

Projections

[1] General government expenditure excluding privatisation proceeds and lottery-financed spending and net of interest and dividend receipts.

Changes since the last Budget

4.25   Tables 4.6, 4.7 and 4.8 summarise changes in the fiscal projections since the last Budget. More detail for 1995–96 and 1996–97 is given in Table 4A.7 of Annex A.

PSBR in 1994–95 and 1995–96

4.26   The outturn for the PSBR in 1994–95 was £1·6 billion higher than the forecast made in the last Budget. Receipts were £2½ billion lower than forecast, but this was partly offset by lower expenditure. Over half the shortfall on receipts was accounted for by lower VAT; income and corporation tax receipts were also lower than forecast. The lower level of receipts has carried through into 1995–96, where the forecast of general government receipts has been revised downwards by nearly £7 billion. Again, lower VAT is the most important single factor; corporation tax has also been revised significantly downwards. Lower receipts are partly explained by lower money GDP, but this does not explain all the shortfall. The composition of spending and of income may also be part of the explanation, but at this stage it is difficult to know the full story. Expenditure is as forecast in the last Budget, leaving the PSBR forecast for 1995–96 between £6½ and £7 billion higher (after adjusting for classification changes).

Table 4.6   Changes in the projections since 1994 Budget[1]

	£ billion					
	1994–95	1995–96	1996–97[2]	1997–98[2]	1998–99[2]	1999–2000[2]
PSBR path in 1994 Budget[1]	**34·3**	**22·3**	**14**	**5**	**–1**	**–9**
Changes in:						
GGE(X)[3]	–1·8	–0·1	–3½	–3½	–3	–3½
general government receipts	–2·6	–6·8	–12½	–12	–9	–9
other items[4]	+0·8	–	–½	+1½	+½	+½
Total change in PSBR	**+1·6**	**+6·7**	**+8½**	**+10**	**+6**	**+6**
PSBR path in 1995 Budget	**35·9**	**29·0**	**22½**	**15**	**5**	**–2**

[1] *In this and other tables in this Chapter, 1994 Budget figures are after allowing for the 8 December 1994 package of measures and after adjusting for classification changes (see paragraph 6A.8).*
[2] *From 1996–97 onwards, changes rounded to nearest £½ billion, except for PSBR from 1997–98, rounded to nearest £1 billion.*
[3] *General government expenditure excluding privatisation proceeds and lottery-financed spending, and net of interest and dividend receipts. See Table 4.8.*
[4] *Lottery-financed spending (+ sign), debt interest receipts (+), privatisation proceeds (–) and public corporations' market and overseas borrowing (+).*

The projections   **4.27**   The PSBR projections are higher throughout than in the last Budget. This is more than explained by lower receipts than previously forecast. General government receipts over the next four years are down by amounts between £9 and £12 billion a year. The Budget tax reductions are worth between £3 and £5 billion a year, and reduce the ratio of receipts to GDP by around ½ to ¾ percentage point. From 1996–97 onwards, the ratio is down by rather more than this – around 1¼ to 1½ percentage points in each year. This reflects the lower level of tax receipts relative to money GDP seen in 1994–95 and 1995–96, which is projected to continue.

4.28   Expenditure is down on last year's Budget projections. The cash reductions of £3 to £4½ billion in Control Total spending announced in the Budget are partly offset by higher debt interest, from higher levels of borrowing. So GGE(X) is down by £3 to £3½ billion a year.

4.29   The reductions in spending announced in the Budget mean that the ratio of spending (GGE(X)) to money GDP is lower throughout than in the 1994 Budget projections.

Table 4.7 Changes in the projection of receipts[1]

	£ billion			
	1996–97	1997–98	1998–99	1999–2000
Current prices				
Budget measures to tax/NICs[2]	−3	−4½	−5	−5
Other changes to tax/NICs	−9	−7	−3	−3
Changes to other receipts	−½	−½	−1	−1
Total change in GGR[3]	**−12½**	**−12**	**−9**	**−9**
1994–95 prices				
Total change in GGR[3]	**−11**	**−11**	**−8½**	**−8½**
Change in GGR/GDP ratio − per cent	−1½	−1½	−1¼	−1¼

[1] *Rounded to the nearest £½ billion.*
[2] *Changes from indexed base. See Tables 1.5 and 5.1.*
[3] *General government receipts.*

Table 4.8 Changes in the public spending projections[1]

	£ billion			
	1996–97	1997–98	1998–99	1999–2000
Current prices				
Control Total	−3	−3½	−4½	−5
Cyclical social security	0	−½	0	0
Central government debt interest	+½	+2	+2	+2
Accounting adjustments	−1	−2	−½	0
GGE(X)[2]	**−3½**	**−3½**	**−3**	**3½**
Privatisation proceeds[3]	−1	−½	−½	0
Other adjustments[4]	+½	+½	+½	+½
Total change in GGE	**−4**	**−3½**	**−3**	**−3**
1994-95 prices				
Control Total	−2½	−3	−4½	−5
Cyclical social security	0	−½	−½	0
Central government debt interest	+½	+2	+2	+1½
Accounting adjustments	−½	−1½	−½	0
GGE(X)[2]	**−2½**	**−3**	**−3½**	**−4**
Privatisation proceeds[3]	−1	−½	−½	0
Other adjustments[4]	+½	+½	+½	+½
Total change in GGE	**−3**	**−3**	**−3½**	**−3½**
Change in GGE(X)[2]/GDP ratio − per cent	−½	−½	−½	−½

[1] *Rounded to the nearest £½ billion.*
[2] *Excluding privatisation proceeds, and lottery-financed spending and net of interest receipts.*
[3] *A minus sign indicates higher privatisation proceeds.*
[4] *Lottery-financed spending and interest and dividend receipts.*

Funding policy

4.30   Funding policy will be carried out on the basis set out in the gilts remit to the Bank of England (published on 30 March 1995) and the Report of the Debt Management Review (published with the Bank of England on 19 July 1995). Table 4.9 updates the funding arithmetic to allow for the new PSBR forecast and the latest information on gilts sales and assumption for net National Savings inflows and other funding. It is now anticipated that £14·9 billion of gilts sales will be required in the months November 1995 to March 1996 for full funding.

4.31   Remits for gilts and National Savings will be published just before the start of the financial year 1996–97. These will explain in more detail the structure of the 1996–97 borrowing programme and how it will be implemented.

Table 4.9   Funding requirement forecast for 1995–96

	£ billion
PSBR	**29·0**
Gilts maturing	4·1
Plus Cumulative underfund	1·4
Funding requirement	**34·6**
Less Net National Savings inflow	−3·0
Less Other funding	−0·5
Gilts sales required for full funding	**31·1**
Less Gilts sales (April – October 1995)	−16·2
Further gilts sales required (November – March 1995–96) for full funding	**14·9**

Margins of Error and alternative projections

Average errors   **4.32**   Given that the PSBR is in essence the difference between two large aggregates it is not surprising that PSBR forecasts are subject to a wide margin of error. Over the past ten years the average absolute error on forecasts of the current year made in the Autumn (November Budget forecasts for the past two years, Autumn Statement forecast for previous years) has averaged ¾ per cent of GDP, equivalent to plus or minus £5½ billion in today's prices. The average absolute error in projections for the year ahead, adjusted for subsequent Budget measures, is 1½ per cent of GDP, or plus or minus £11 billion in today's prices.

Alternative projections   **4.33**   There are inevitably uncertainties about the path of the economy in the medium term; and a different output profile from the main projection described in Chapter 3 would affect the outlook for the public finances.

Table 4.10   Variant GDP[1] growth projections

	1996–97	1997–98	1998–99	1999–00	2000–01
Main case	3	3	2¾	2¾	2¾
Higher growth	3½	3½	3¼	3¼	3¼
Lower growth	2½	2½	2¼	2¼	2¼

[1] *Non-oil GDP.*

4.34   Tax revenues and some parts of government expenditure (such as cyclical social security) vary automatically with cycles in economic activity. This sensitivity is illustrated below using the relationships set out in the recently published study[1] of the effects of the cycle on the public finances. The variant growth projections in Table 4.10 differ from the main projection by ½ per cent in either direction from 1996–97.

4.35   Table 4.11 shows the path of the PSBR on unchanged policies in these alternative projections. Public expenditure within the Control Total is unchanged, but cyclical social security and debt interest payments are allowed to vary. Tax rates, allowances and thresholds are kept at the same levels as in the main projection, with revenues allowed to vary with the path of output.

Table 4.11   Variant PSBR projections

	Per cent of GDP				
	1996–97	1997–98	1998–99	1999–00	2000–01
Main case	3	2	¾	–¼	–1½
Higher growth	2¾	1½	–¼	–1½	–3
Lower growth	3	2½	1½	1	0

4.36   In the higher growth projection the PSBR is eliminated a year earlier than in the main projection. Even in the lower growth case, budget balance is achieved by the end of the period.

[1] *HM Treasury Occasional Paper No.4 "Public Finances and the Cycle".*

Annex A to Chapter 4
Further analyses of the public finances

4A.1 This annex contains a number of further analyses of the forecast of the public finances in 1995–96 and 1996–97. There are also two tables which set out historical series for the PSBR and its main components, including general government expenditure and general government receipts.

4A.2 The following analyses are included:

(i) **General government receipts** – further tax-by-tax details of the forecasts for 1995–96 and 1996–97 (Table 4A.1);

(ii) **Sectoral breakdown of PSBR** forecasts for 1995–96 (Table 4A.2);

(iii) **Central government transactions on a cash basis** – forecasts for 1995–96 and 1996–97 (Table 4A.3);

(iv) **Economic category analyses of local authority and public corporations transactions** (Tables 4A.4 and 4A.5);

(v) **A full analysis of receipts and expenditure by economic category** for 1995–96 and 1996–97 (Table 4A.6);

(vi) **Changes to PSBR forecasts** for 1995–96 and 1996–97 since the last Budget and since the Summer Economic Forecast (Table 4A.7);

(vii) **Historical series for the PSBR and its main components** (Tables 4A.8 and 4A.9).

Table 4A.1 General government receipts[1]

	£ billion			
	1994–95	1995–96		1996–97
	Outturn	Last Budget forecast	Latest forecast	Forecast
Inland Revenue				
Income tax	63·1	70·1	68·9	70·2
Corporation tax[2]	19·4	26·4	24·7	26·6
Petroleum revenue tax	0·7	0·7	0·9	1·0
Capital gains tax	0·9	0·8	0·9	1·0
Inheritance tax	1·4	1·5	1·5	1·5
Stamp duties	1·8	2·0	2·0	2·4
Total Inland Revenue	**87·3**	**101·5**	**98·8**	**102·6**
Customs and Excise				
Value added tax	41·8	48·1	44·0	47·9
Fuel duties	14·0	16·0	15·5	17·4
Tobacco duties	7·4	7·2	7·2	7·7
Spirits duties	1·8	1·7	1·6	1·7
Wine duties	1·1	1·2	1·2	1·2
Beer and cider duties	2·6	2·7	2·7	2·8
Betting and gaming duties	1·2	1·2	1·6	1·7
Customs duties	2·0	2·1	2·3	2·4
Agricultural levies	0·2	0·2	0·1	0·2
Air passenger duty	0·1	0·3	0·3	0·3
Insurance premium tax	0·1	0·7	0·6	0·7
Landfill tax				0·1
Total Customs and Excise	**72·3**	**81·3**	**77·4**	**84·1**
Vehicle excise duties	3·8	4·0	4·1	4·3
Oil royalties	0·5	0·5	0·6	0·5
Business rates[3]	12·7	13·8	13·6	14·7
Social security contributions	42·1	44·6	44·4	46·9
Council tax	9·1	9·2	9·2	9·9
Other taxes and royalties	6·0	5·8	6·2	5·7
Total taxes and social security contributions	**233·7**	**260·9**	**254·2**	**268·7**
Interest and dividends	5·0	4·6	5·2	4·8
Gross trading surpluses and rent	5·0	5·7	5·2	5·3
Other receipts[4]	6·4	7·6	7·3	6·0
General government receipts	**250·0**	**278·7**	**271·9**	**284·8**
North Sea revenues[5]	1·6	2·2	2·3	3·0

[1] *On a cash basis. See Annex B.*

[2] *Includes advance corporation tax (net of repayments): 8·1 8·6 9·9 9·4 (also includes North Sea corporation tax after ACT set-off, and corporation tax on gains).*

[3] *Includes district council rates in Northern Ireland.*

[4] *Includes payments into the National Lottery Distribution Fund and accruals adjustments for index-linked gilts.*

[5] *North Sea corporation tax (before ACT set-off), petroleum revenue tax and oil royalties.*

Borrowing by sector   **4A.3**   Central government borrowing on its own account (ie excluding borrowing for on-lending to local authorities and public corporations) more than accounted for the total PSBR in 1994–95 and is expected to do so again in 1995–96. Central government borrowing on its own account in the first seven months of 1995–96 was £2½ billion lower than in the same period of 1994–95. The forecast for 1995–96 as a whole implies borrowing in November to March which is over £4 billion lower than in the same period last year.

Table 4A.2   Public sector borrowing requirement by sector

	£ billion					
	1994–95			1995–96		
	Outturn			Outturn	Forecast	
	Apr–Oct	Nov–Mar	Total	Apr–Oct	Nov–Mar	Total
CGBR(O)[1]	21·8	16·5	38·3	19·3	12·3	31·6
LABR[2]	−0·8	−0·1	−1·0	0·7	−0·7	0·1
PCBR[3]	−1·4	0·0	−1·4	−1·3	−1·4	−2·7
PSBR	**19·6**	**16·3**	**35·9**	**18·8**	**10·2**	**29·0**
CGBR[4]	20·6	17·8	38·3	19·8	10·0	29·8

[1] *Central government borrowing requirement on its own account.*

[2] *Local authority borrowing requirement.*

[3] *Public corporations' borrowing requirement.*

[4] *Central government borrowing requirement, including on-lending to local authorities and public corporations.*

4A.4   Local authorities made a net repayment of £1·0 billion in 1994–95; a marginal borrowing requirement is forecast for 1995–96. Public corporations made a net repayment of £1·4 billion in 1994–95; the forecast is for a larger repayment in 1995–96.

Central government transactions on a cash basis   **4A.5**   The monthly outturns for central government borrowing are measured from the cash flows into and out of central government's funds and accounts, after consolidation. Table 4A.3 sets out the 1994–95 outturn and 1995–96 and 1996–97 forecasts for central government borrowing in terms of this cash flow presentation.

Table 4A.3   Central government transactions on a cash receipts and outlays basis

	£ billion			
	1994–95	1995–96		1996–97
	Outturn	Last Budget forecast	Latest forecast	Forecast
Receipts				
Inland Revenue[1]	87·3	101·5	98·8	102·6
Customs and Excise[1]	72·5	81·5	77·6	84·4
Social security contributions (GB)	40·7	43·1	42·9	45·3
Interest and dividends	7·8	7·8	8·1	7·8
Other	17·3	18·8	19·7	19·8
Total receipts	**225·5**	**252·6**	**247·2**	**259·9**
Outlays				
Interest payments	21·4	23·0	23·5	26·6
Privatisation proceeds	−6·4	−3·0	−3·0	−4·0
Net department outlays	248·9	258·5[2]	258·4	262·5[2]
Total outlays	**263·8**	**278·4[2]**	**278·8**	**285·1[2]**
Net own account borrowing[3]	**38·3**	**25·9[2]**	**31·6**	**25·3[2]**
Net lending to local authorities and public corporations	0·1	−1·6	−1·8	−1·1
Net borrowing	**38·3**	**24·2[3]**	**29·8**	**24·1[2]**

[1] *Payments to the Consolidated Fund.*
[2] *Assumes Reserve allocated to central government sector.*
[3] *Excludes net lending to local authorities and public corporations.*

Public finances by economic category

4A.6   Table 4A.6 shows a full analysis of receipts and expenditure by economic category with a breakdown between central government, local authorities and public corporations. Annex B explains the conventions used, which follow in most respects those in the UK national income and expenditure accounts.

4A.7   The table makes the assumption that the Reserve for 1996–97 is spent entirely on transactions that fall above the financial deficit line, although in practice allocations from the Reserve can also affect financial transactions. The Reserve for 1996–97 has been further apportioned between current and capital expenditure, on the basis of the experience of past outturns. It has also been assumed that all of the Reserve will be spent by central government; in practice allocations from the Reserve can be made to local authorities and public corporations spending as well.

4A.8   Tables 4A.4 and 4A.5 summarises the information on local authorities' and public corporations' transactions in Table 4A.6, and also provide outturn figures for 1994–95.

Table 4A.4   Local authority transactions

	£ billion		
	Outturn	Forecast	
	1994–95	1995–96	1996–97
Receipts			
Council tax[1]	8·8	9·1	10·0
Current grants from central government	56·5	57·2	58·4
Other receipts[2]	7·3	7·8	7·9
Capital grants from central government	2·8	3·3	3·3
Total receipts	**75·3**	**77·5**	**79·6**
Expenditure			
Current expenditure on goods and services	51·8	52·6	54·0
Current grants and subsidies	13·8	14·1	14·7
Interest	4·2	4·1	4·1
Capital expenditure before depreciation	7·1	7·7	6·3
Total expenditure	**76·8**	**78·4**	**79·2[3]**
Financial deficit	**1·5**	**1·0**	**−0·4**
Net financial transactions	−2·4	−0·9	−0·5
Net borrowing	**−1·0**	**0·1**	**−1·0**

[1] *Net of rebates and council tax benefit. Includes district council rates in Northern Ireland shown in "Taxes on expenditure" in Table 4A.6 (line 2).*
[2] *Includes interest receipts, rent and gross trading surplus.*
[3] *Assumes no allocation from the Reserve.*

Table 4A.5   Public corporations' transactions

	£ billion		
	Outturn	Forecast	
	1994–95	1995–96	1996–97
Receipts			
Gross trading surplus (including subsidies)	4·7	5·5	5·4
Other current grants	0·9	1·0	1·0
Capital grants from general government	3·5	4·2	2·4
Total receipts	**9·0**	**10·6**	**8·8**
Expenditure			
Interest, dividends and taxes on income	2·4	2·6	2·4
Capital expenditure before depreciation	5·2	6·0	5·8
Total expenditure	**7·7**	**8·6**	**8·1[1]**
Financial deficit	**−1·3**	**−2·0**	**−0·7**
Net financial transactions	−0·1	−0·7	−1·2
Net borrowing	**−1·4**	**−2·7**	**−1·9**

[1] *Assumes no allocation from the Reserve.*

Table 4A.6 Public sector transactions by sub–sector and economic category

		£ billion				
		1995–96				
		General government				
	Line[1]	Central government	Local authorities	Total	Public corporations	Public sector
Current receipts[2]						
Taxes on income and royalties	1	96·0	0·0	96·0	−0·2	95·9
Taxes on expenditure	2	104·1	0·2	104·3	0·0	104·3
Taxes on capital	3	2·5	0·0	2·5	0·0	2·5
Social security contributions	4	44·6	0·0	44·6	0·0	44·6
Council tax	5	0·0	9·0	9·0	0·0	9·0
Gross trading surplus	6	−0·1	0·8	0·8	5·5	6·2
Rent and miscellaneous current transfers	7	2·4	4·2	6·7	0·4	7·1
Interest and dividends from private sector and abroad	8	2·3	0·6	2·9	0·2	3·2
Interest and dividends within public sector	9	5·8	−3·5	2·3	−2·3	0·0
Imputed charge for non-trading capital consumption	10	1·3	2·0	3·4	0·0	3·4
Total current receipts	11	**259·2**	**13·3**	**272·4**	**3·7**	**276·1**
Current expenditure[2]						
Current expenditure on goods and services	12	97·0	52·6	149·6	0·0	149·6
Depreciation	13	2·1	4·5	6·7	3·5	10·2
Subsidies	14	7·0	0·7	7·7	0·0	7·7
Current grants to personal sector	15	82·7	13·4	96·1	0·0	96·1
Current grants abroad	16	6·3	0·0	6·3	0·0	6·3
Current grants within public sector	17	57·2	−57·2	0·0	0·0	0·0
Debt interest	18	25·1	0·5[3]	25·6	−0·2[3]	25·5
Apportionment of Reserve	19					
Total current expenditure	20	**277·4**	**14·6**	**292·0**	**3·3**	**295·3**
Current deficit	21	**18·2**	**1·3**	**19·6**	**−0·4**	**19·2**
Capital transfers	22		**0·2**	**0·2**	**−0·1**	**0·1**
Capital expenditure[2]						
Gross domestic fixed capital expenditure	23	5·6	6·4	11·9	5·7	17·6
Less Depreciation	24	−2·1	−4·5	−6·7	−3·5	−10·2
Increase in stocks	25	−0·1	0·0	−0·1	−0·2	−0·3
Capital grants to private sector	26	3·4	1·3	4·7	0·4	5·1
Capital grants to public sector	27	7·5	−3·3	4·2	−4·2	0·0
Apportionment of Reserve	28					
Total capital expenditure	29	**14·2**	**−0·2**	**14·0**	**−1·7**	**12·3**
Financial deficit	30	**32·5**	**1·0**	**33·4**	**−2·0**	**1·4**
Financial transactions						
Net lending to private sector and abroad	31	0·8	−0·2	0·7	0·0	0·7
Cash expenditure on company securities (including privatisation proceeds)	32	−3·0	0·0	−3·1	0·0	−3·1
Transactions concerning certain public sector pension schemes	33	1·1	0·0	1·1	0·0	1·1
Accruals adjustments on receipts	34	2·7	−0·4	2·3	0·0	2·3
Other accruals adjustments	35	−1·6	0·0	−1·6	−0·9	−2·5
Miscellaneous financial transactions	36	−0·7	−0·3	−1·0	−0·1	−0·9
Borrowing requirement	37	**31·6[4]**	**0·1**	**31·7**	**−2·7**	**29·0**

[1] *Current deficit (line 21) = current expenditure (line 20) − current receipts (line 11).*

Financial deficit (line 30) = current deficit (line 21) − capital receipts (line 22) + capital expenditure (line 29).

[2] *On an accruals basis.*

[3] *Excluding local authorities' payments to central government and public corporations' payments to general government, which are in line 9.*

[4] *Own account borrowing.*

Table 4A.6   Public sector transactions by sub-sector and economic category – *continued*

£ billion

1996–97

Line[1]	General government			Public corporations	Public sector	
	Central government	Local authorities	Total			
						Current receipts[2]
1	99·0	0·0	99·0	−0·2	98·8	Taxes on income and royalties
2	116·6	0·2	111·7	0·0	111·7	Taxes on expenditure
3	2·8	0·0	2·8	0·0	2·8	Taxes on capital
4	47·0	0·0	47·0	0·0	47·0	Social security contributions
5	0·0	9·8	9·8	0·0	9·8	Council tax
6	−0·1	0·8	0·8	5·4	6·1	Gross trading surplus
7	2·5	4·2	6·7	0·5	7·3	Rent and miscellaneous current transfers
8	2·1	0·6	2·8	0·2	3·0	Interest and dividends from private sector and abroad
9	5·6	−3·6	2·0	−2·0	0·0	Interest and dividends within public sector
10	1·4	2·1	3·5	0·0	3·5	Imputed charge for non-trading capital consumption
11	**271·9**	**14·1**	**286·0**	**3·9**	**289·9**	**Total current receipts**
						Current expenditure[2]
12	98·4	54·0	152·4	0·0	152·4	Current expenditure on goods and services
13	2·2	4·7	6·9	3·6	10·5	Depreciation
14	6·8	0·7	7·3	0·0	7·5	Subsidies
15	85·8	14·0	99·8	0·0	99·8	Current grants to personal sector
16	6·2	0·0	6·2	0·0	6·2	Current grants abroad
17	58·4	−58·4	0·0	0·0	0·0	Current grants within public sector
18	26·5	0·5[3]	27·0	−0·2[3]	26·9	Debt interest
19	2·2	0·0	2·2	0·0	2·2	Apportionment of Reserve
20	**286·5**	**15·6**	**302·1**	**3·4**	**305·5**	**Total current expenditure**
21	**14·6**	**1·4**	**16·0**	**−0·5**	**15·5**	**Current deficit**
22	**0·0**	**0·2**	**0·2**	**−0·1**	**0·1**	**Capital transfers**
						Capital expenditure[2]
23	4·7	5·2	9·9	5·3	15·2	Gross domestic fixed capital expenditure
24	−2·2	−4·7	−6·9	−3·6	−10·5	*Less* Depreciation
25	−0·1	0·0	−0·1	0·0	−0·1	Increase in stocks
26	3·5	1·1	4·7	0·4	5·0	Capital grants to private sector
27	5·7	−3·3	2·4	−2·4	0·0	Capital grants to public sector
28	0·3	0·0	0·3	0·0	0·3	Apportionment of Reserve
29	**12·2**	**−1·7**	**10·3**	**−0·3**	**10·0**	**Total capital expenditure**
30	**26·5**	**−0·4**	**26·1**	**−0·7**	**25·4**	**Financial deficit**
						Financial transactions
31	1·0	−0·1	0·8	0·0	0·8	Net lending to private sector and abroad
32	−4·0	0·0	−4·0	0·0	−4·0	Cash expenditure on company securities (including privatisation proceeds)
33	0·7	0·0	0·7	0·0	0·7	Transactions concerning certain public sector pension schemes
34	1·6	−0·1	1·6	0·0	1·6	Accruals adjustments on receipts
35	0·1	0·0	0·1	−1·1	−1·0	Other accruals adjustments
36	−0·7	−0·3	−1·0	−0·1	−1·1	Miscellaneous financial transactions
37	**25·3[4]**	**−1·0**	**24·3**	**−1·9**	**22·4**	**Borrowing requirement**

Changes to forecasts **4A.9** Table 4A.7 provides details of changes to the public finance forecasts for 1995–96 and 1996–97 since the last Budget and since the Summer Economic Forecast. Previous forecasts have been adjusted for subsequent classification changes (see Annex A to Chapter 6, paragraph 6A.8). Tax-by-tax details of the effects of the Budget measures are set out in Table 5.1, and a breakdown of the Control Total changes by department is shown in Table 6.6.

Table 4A.7   Comparison with previous forecasts[1]

	£ billion			
	Changes since last Budget		Changes since Summer Economic Forecast	
	1995–96	1996–97	1995–96	1996–97
Expenditure				
Control Total	−0·8	−3·2	−0·8	−3·2
Other general government expenditure[2]	+1·1	+0·2	+1·1	+0·6
Public corporations' market and overseas borrowing	−0·4	+0·2	−0·1	−0·2
Privatisation proceeds[3]	0·0	−1·0	0·0	0·0
Total expenditure	**−0·1**	**−3·9**	**+0·1**	**−2·8**
Receipts				
Inland Revenue	−2·7	−8·4	−1·6	−6·2
Customs and Excise	−3·9	−3·1	−2·0	−0·7
Social security contributions	−0·2	−0·1	+0·1	+0·2
Other receipts	0·0	−0·7	−1·0	−1·9
Total receipts	**−6·8**	**−12·3**	**−4·5**	**−8·5**
PSBR	**+6·7**	**+8·4**	**+4·6**	**+5·7**

[1] *Previous forecasts have been adjusted for classification changes.*
[2] *Excluding privatisation proceeds.*
[3] *A minus sign indicates higher privatisation proceeds.*

Historical series for the PSBR and its main components

4A.10 Table 4A.8 sets out historical series for the PSBR and its main components, including GGE(X), as shown in Chart 4.4. Table 4A.9 shows further details for Government receipts, including the historical series for total taxes and social security contributions shown in Chart 4.3.

Table 4A.8 Historical series for the PSBR and its components

	Per cent of money GDP					
	GGE(X)	Other GGE	GGE	General government receipts	Public corporations' market and overseas borrowing	**PSBR**
1965–66	36½	1½	37¾	35¼	0	**2¾**
1966–67	38	1½	39½	36¼	0	**3**
1967–68	41½	1½	43¼	38	-¼	**5**
1968–69	40	1¾	41½	40¾	0	**¾**
1969–70	39¼	1¾	41	41¾	-½	**-1¼**
1970–71	39½	1¾	41¼	40¼	½	**1½**
1971–72	40	1¾	41¾	39¾	-¼	**1¾**
1972–73	39¾	1¾	41½	38	0	**3¾**
1973–74	41½	2	43½	38½	1	**6**
1974–75	46¾	2	48¾	40½	¾	**9**
1975–76	47¼	2	49¼	40¼	¼	**9½**
1976–77	44¾	2	46¾	41	¾	**6½**
1977–78	41½	1½	43	39¾	¼	**3½**
1978–79	42¼	1¾	44	38¾	¼	**5½**
1979–80	42½	1½	44	38¾	-¼	**4¾**
1980–81	44¾	1¾	46½	40¾	-½	**5¼**
1981–82	45½	1¾	47	43¾	0	**3¼**
1982–83	45½	1¾	47¼	43¾	-½	**3¼**
1983–84	44¾	1¼	46¼	42¾	0	**3¼**
1984–85	45¼	1	46¼	43½	¼	**3**
1985–86	43¼	1	44¼	42¼	-¼	**1½**
1986–87	42¼	¼	42¾	41½	-¼	**1**
1987–88	40½	¼	40¾	41	-¼	**-¾**
1988–89	38	-¼	37¾	40¼	-½	**-3**
1989–90	38¼	½	38¾	40	-¼	**-1½**
1990–91	39	¼	39¼	39¼	0	**0**
1991–92	41	-½	40¾	38¼	0	**2¼**
1992–93	43½	-½	43	36¾	-¼	**6**
1993–94	43½	0	43¼	36	-¼	**7**
1994–95	42¾	-¼	42½	37	-¼	**5¼**
1995–96	42	¼	42½	38¼	-¼	**4**
1996–97	40½	¼	41	37¾	-¼	**3**
1997–98	39¾	½	40¼	38¼	0	**2**
1998–99	38¾	½	39¼	38½	0	**¾**
1999–00	38	½	38½	38¾	0	**-¼**
2000–01	37	½	37¼	39	0	**-1½**

Table 4A.9 Historical series for government receipts

	Per cent of money GDP				
	Total taxes and NICs	Other receipts	**General government receipts**	Non-North Sea taxes and NICs[1]	Public sector current receipts
1965–66	31¾	3½	**35¼**	31¾	37½
1966–67	32½	3¾	**36¼**	32½	38¼
1967–68	34	4	**38**	34	39¾
1968–69	35¾	5	**40¾**	35¾	42
1969–70	37½	4¼	**41¾**	37½	43¾
1970–71	37	3¼	**40¼**	37	42¾
1971–72	35¼	4½	**39¾**	35¼	41
1972–73	33	5	**38**	33	38¾
1973–74	33¾	4¾	**38½**	33¾	40
1974–75	36¼	4¼	**40½**	36¼	43
1975–76	36¾	3½	**40¼**	36¾	43¼
1976–77	36¼	4¾	**41**	36½	43¾
1977–78	35¼	4½	**39¾**	35½	42
1978–79	34¼	4½	**38¾**	34¾	41
1979–80	35½	3¼	**38¾**	35½	41¾
1980–81	36¾	4	**40¾**	36½	43
1981–82	39¾	3¾	**43¾**	39¼	46½
1982–83	39½	4¼	**43¾**	38½	46
1983–84	39	3¾	**42¾**	38¼	45
1984–85	39¾	3¾	**43½**	38¼	44½
1985–86	38¾	3½	**42¼**	37¼	44
1986–87	38¼	3¼	**41½**	37¾	42¾
1987–88	38¼	2¾	**41**	38	42½
1988–89	37½	2¾	**40¼**	37¼	41½
1989–90	37	3	**40**	37	40¾
1990–91	37	2¼	**39¼**	37	39¾
1991–92	36½	2	**38¼**	36¾	39
1992–93	34½	2¼	**36¾**	34¾	37¼
1993–94	34	2¼	**36**	34	36¼
1994–95	35	2	**37**	35¼	37½
1995–96	36	2¼	**38¼**	36¼	38¾
1996–97	35¾	2	**37¾**	36	38½
1997–98	36¼	2	**38¼**	36½	38¾
1998–99	36¾	1¾	**38½**	37	39¼
1999–00	37	1¾	**38¾**	37¼	39¼
2000–01	37¼	1¾	**39**	37½	39½

[1] *As a percent of non-North Sea GDP.*

Annex B to Chapter 4
Conventions used in presenting the public finances

4B.1 The FSBR presents the public finances in two main ways; on a cash basis and on a national accounts, or accruals, basis. This Annex briefly describes the two approaches and outlines the relationships between the various public finances tables in Chapters 1, 4, 5 and 6.

4B.2 An important point to note at the outset is that the key expenditure and receipts aggregates, general government expenditure (GGE) and general government receipts (GGR), are concepts derived from national accounts definitions. But they can be disaggregated on both a national accounts basis and on a largely cash basis.

Cash basis

4B.3 The cash approach concentrates on the actual cash transactions between the public sector and the rest of the economy in any given period of time. It is particularly useful for analysing the components of the PSBR, which is itself almost entirely a cash concept. A cash basis also corresponds closely to the way public expenditure is planned, controlled and accounted for at present.

Tables 1.7, 4.1, 4.4, 4.5, **4B.4** The main – albeit summary – presentation of the public finances on a cash basis
4A.1 and 6.3 is given in Tables 1.7 and 4.1. Supporting disaggregation of general government expenditure is given in Tables 4.5 and 6.3, while Tables 4.4 and 4A.1 provide further breakdowns of general government receipts. Table 1.7 is a more detailed presentation of the public finances for the current year and year ahead.

4B.5 As far as possible, the figures in these tables relate to actual cash flows. The estimates of taxes for example are for tax payments received during the year, rather than for liabilities incurred. There are however, a number of items which are not on a cash basis:

- "social security contributions" are scored gross of amounts netted off by employers as reimbursement in respect of statutory sick pay and statutory maternity pay. These payments count as expenditure rather than negative receipts;

- VAT refunded to central and local government is included in "other taxes and royalties" (Table 4.4, Table 4A.1 and Table 1.7);

- an imputed flow for capital consumption by general government is included in "other receipts" (Table 4.4, Table 4A.1 and Table 1.7).

These latter two flows have no impact on the PSBR as they also appear on the expenditure side of the account in "accounting adjustments" (Table 1.7). This line also includes various other adjustments needed to get back to the national accounts basis required for GGE.

4B.6 The final departure from a cash basis is the "central government debt interest" line of Table 1.7, which scores the capital uplift on index-linked gilts as interest at the time it accrues. Because the PSBR is on a cash basis, an offset is made in the form of an accruals adjustment to "other receipts" (Table 4A.1, Table 4.4 and Table 1.7). This removes the accrued uplift scored and adds back any actual payments of uplift on redemptions.

4B.7 Tables 1.6 and 4.5 are on the same basis as Table 1.7.

Table 4A.3   **4B.8** The other cash-based table is Table 4A.3, which shows the finances of central government. Unlike the earlier tables this is genuinely a cash presentation based on information from central government funds and accounts. The inputed flows for refunded VAT, social security contributions and capital consumption are all excluded, and the "interest payments" line takes account of actual payments of capital uplift on index-linked gilts, rather than the accrued uplift.

4B.9 Similar tables cannot be produced for local authorities or public corporations because the available cash data are not comprehensive. The finances of these sectors, shown in Tables 4A.4 and 4A.5, are presented on the national accounts basis described below.

National accounts basis

4B.10 The national accounts are produced by the CSO for the UK as a whole using an internationally agreed framework. Public finances shown on this basis can thus be placed more easily into the context of the rest of the economy, highlighting the inter-relationships between different sectors.

Table 4A.6   **4B.11** Table 4A.6 gives a detailed national accounts presentation of the short-term forecasts for the public finances. Under the measurement conventions used in the national accounts:

- most transactions, including most taxes (although not corporation tax), are recorded on an accruals rather than a cash payment basis;

- transactions are grouped by economic category. So, for example, transfer payments are distinguished from expenditure on goods and services;

- the value of some transactions is imputed where no money changes hands (for example, non-trading capital consumption).

4B.12   The public sector financial deficit is the balance between expenditure and income in the combined current and capital accounts (line 30 of Table 4A.6). Unlike the PSBR, the financial deficit is not wholly a measure of cash transactions because certain items above line 30 are measured on an accruals basis. The appropriate accruals adjustments are made in lines 34 and 35. Certain other financial transactions, notably net lending and privatisation proceeds are also excluded from the financial deficit, but included in the PSBR.

4B.13   As the national accounts distinguish between current and capital transactions, they provide the natural framework in which to identify the current balance and capital spending. The current and capital breakdown shown in Table 4A.6 differs from the usual national accounts conventions in two respects. First, capital taxes (line 3) are counted as current rather than capital receipts on the grounds that they are not strictly speaking pure taxes on capital. And second, an estimate of depreciation is deducted from capital expenditure and added to current expenditure.

4B.14   GGE can be derived from the general government column of Table 4A.6 by taking current expenditure (line 20) plus capital expenditure (line 29) and adding:

- the Reserve (lines 19 and 28, all assumed to be general government);

- net lending to the private sector and abroad (line 31);

- cash expenditure on company securities (line 32);

- and net lending by central government to public corporations (minus £1·5 billion in 1995–96 and minus £0·8 billion in 1996–97).

4B.15   Correspondingly, GGR comprises general government current receipts (line 11) plus capital transfers (line 22), less:

- transactions concerning public sector pension schemes (line 33);

- accruals adjustments (lines 34 and 35);

- miscellaneous financial transactions (line 36).

Tables 1.1 and 4.2   **4B.16**   A summary version of the public sector column of Table 4A.6 provides the framework for Tables 1.1 and 4.2. So, for example, receipts and current expenditure in these tables correspond to lines 11 and 20 of Table 4A.6. "Public sector net capital spending" represents the balance on the capital account: that is, total capital expenditure (line 29 of Table 4A.6) net of capital transfers (line 22). GGE and GGR cannot be derived from Table 1.1 because it show figures for the public sector, rather than just general government, and because it gives insufficient detail of the various financial transactions. Table 4.2 also shows as a memorandum item the general government financial deficit, which appears as line 30 of the general government column of Table 4A.6.

4B.17   Tables 1.1 and 4.2 show the current balance in the same way as Table 4A.6. Tables 4A.4 and 4A.5 are also on a national accounts basis.

4B.18   Tables 1.1 and 4.2 show projections of the public finances over the period to 2000–01. A detailed breakdown in the form of Table 4A.6 is, however, only provided for 1995–96 and 1996–97.

Table 4A.9   **4B.19**   An accruals basis is used to calculate taxes (and social security contributions and council tax) as a per cent of GDP (Table 4A.9), because this gives a measure of the underlying burden of taxation stemming from a particular period of economic activity. It is not affected, for example, by the precise timing of tax receipts.

Tables 4A.4 and 4A.5   **4B.20**   Table 4A.6 shows local authorities' self-financed expenditure (net of their receipts from central government – line 17) and their receipts from outside the public sector (net of debt interest payments to central government – line 9). Table 4A.4, in contrast, provides figures for total local authority expenditure and receipts. It also gives a summary presentation of the income and expenditure flows in the local authority accounts, which it is not practical to put together from any other sources.

4B.21   Table 4A.5 serves the same purposes for public corporations as Table 4A.4 does for local authorities. Because public corporations are trading bodies, the national accounts presentation is a little different from that for general government. Most current expenditure is netted off from income to leave the gross trading surplus (shown under receipts). The expenditure side of the account only shows interest, dividend and tax payments, plus capital spending.

Borrowing requirements

4B.22   The PSBR can be disaggregated into component borrowing requirements in different ways. Tables 1.7 and 4.1 show the PSBR as the sum of the general government borrowing requirement (GGBR) and market and overseas borrowing by public corporations (PCMOB). An alternative is to split it, as in Table 4A.2 and Table 4A.6 (line 37), between central government borrowing on its own account (the CGBR(O), and borrowing by local authorities and public corporations (the LABR and PCBR respectively). Table 4A.2 also shows, as a memorandum item, the central government borrowing requirement (CGBR), which is the CGBR(O) plus central government net lending to local authorities and public corporations. The borrowing requirement shown in the general government column of Table 4A.6 is not in fact the GGBR, but the GGBR(O). The GGBR can be calculated by adding in public corporations' borrowing from central government (given in paragraph 4B.14).

Public sector debt

4B.23   Table 4.3 sets out projections for two different measures of public sector debt. Net public sector debt is the stock analogue of the PSBR. It measures the public sector's financial liabilities to the private sector and abroad, net of short-term financial assets.

4B.24   Gross general government debt is the measure of debt used in the European Union's excessive deficits procedure. As a general government measure, it excludes the debt of public corporations. It measures general government's total financial liabilities before netting off short-term financial assets.

5 The Budget tax and national insurance measures

5.01 This chapter summarises the tax and national insurance proposals in the Budget[1].

Objectives

5.02 The Government's overall objectives for the tax system are to:

- keep the overall tax burden as low as possible, through firm control over public spending;

- reduce marginal tax rates on income and business profits, to sharpen incentives to work and create wealth through enterprise and investment;

- maintain a broad tax base which helps to keep tax rates low and avoids distorting decisions;

- shift the balance of taxation from taxes on income to taxes on spending;

- simplify the administration of the tax system and minimise the burdens which compliance places on the taxpayer;

- ensure that the tax system is applied fairly and evenly, closing loopholes so that commercial decisions are not distorted by attempts to avoid tax;

- use the tax system to enable markets to work better, for example by making decision makers aware of the external costs of their decisions; and

- thereby raise revenue in ways which do least harm to the economy and take account of the competitive position of UK business.

5.03 The Budget furthers these objectives by:

- cutting taxes overall by £3¼ billion, rising to £4¾ billion in 1998–99, with the bulk of the cuts falling on direct tax;

- reducing the marginal rates of tax for 18 million taxpayers and for 350,000 companies;

- cutting taxes on savings, inheritance and capital gains to encourage thrift and enterprise;

---

[1] *The effect of the measures on government revenues is set out in Table 5.1. Annex A explains the costings and Annex B details a number of tax changes which were announced before the Budget. The number in brackets after each proposal refers to the line in Table 5.1 where its yield or cost is shown. The symbol "−" means the proposal has no effect on revenue. "★" means it has negligible effects on revenue amounting to less than £3 million a year.*

- taking steps to simplify tax, cut compliance costs for business and close loopholes; and

- implementing previously announced measures to raise tax on road fuels and tobacco, and introduce a tax on landfilled waste.

Personal taxation

Income   **5.04**   The Budget proposes three significant steps towards a 20 per cent basic rate of income tax. It:

- cuts the basic rate of income tax from 25 per cent to 24 per cent (7);

- widens the 20 per cent lower rate band by £500 more than indexation, a total increase of £700 (5); and

- cuts the rate of tax on savings income to 20 per cent for basic rate taxpayers (see para. 5.08).

5.05   The Budget also proposes to:

- increase the basic rate limit by £200 more than indexation, a total increase of £1,200 (6);

- increase personal allowances, including allowances for the elderly, by £100 more than indexation (1), (2);

  increase married couple's allowances, the additional personal allowance, the widow's bereavement allowance and relief for maintenance payments (3), and the income limit for age related allowances (4), in line with statutory indexation (based on the 3·9 per cent increase in the RPI in the year to September 1995); and

- increase the blind person's allowance to £1,250 (*).

5.06   These measures will:

- cut tax for 26 million taxpayers, including three million pensioners;

- reduce marginal tax rates for 18 million people;

- ensure that nearly a quarter of all taxpayers pay tax at a marginal rate of no more than 20 per cent; and

- take 220,000 out of tax altogether, relative to indexation.

5.07   The new allowances and bands of taxable income are:

Income tax allowances (£)	1995–96	1996–97	Increase
Personal allowance	3 525	3 765	240
Married couple's allowance, additional personal allowance, widow's bereavement allowance[1]	1 720	1 790	70
For people aged 65–74:			
personal allowance	4 630	4 910	280
married couple's allowance[1]	2 995	3 115	120
For people aged 75 and over:			
personal allowance	4 800	5 090	290
married couple's allowance[1]	3 035	3 155	120
Income limit for age related allowances	14 600	15 200	600
Blind person's allowance	1 200	1 250	50

[1] *Tax relief for these allowances is restricted to 15 per cent.*

Bands of taxable income (£)	1995–96	1996–97	Increase
Lower rate – 20 per cent	0 – 3 200	0 – 3 900	700
Basic rate – 25 per cent	3 201 – 24 300		
– 24 per cent		3 901 – 25 500	
Higher rate – 40 per cent	over 24 300	over 25 500	1 200

Savings   **5.08**   The tax on savings income, such as bank and building society interest, will be reduced from the basic rate to the lower rate of 20 per cent for basic rate taxpayers, from 6 April 1996. The rate at which tax is deducted from interest will also be reduced to 20 per cent. These changes will reduce tax on savings income for some 14 million taxpayers, increasing incentives to save. Lower rate taxpayers will no longer need to reclaim the difference between tax deducted and tax due. Higher rate taxpayers will continue to be liable at 40 per cent on their savings income (8).

Capital   **5.09**   The qualifying age for capital gains tax retirement relief will be reduced from 55 to 50 (9). The CGT annual exempt amount will be indexed (–).

5.10   The threshold for inheritance tax will be increased by £40,000 more than indexation to £200,000, allowing more wealth to be passed between generations free of tax (10).

Allowances and thresholds (£)	1995–96	1996–97	Increase
CGT annual exempt amount:			
individuals	6 000	6 300	300
trustees	3 000	3 150	150
Inheritance tax threshold	154 000	200 000	46 000

5.11 The inheritance tax relief for holdings of unquoted shares in trading companies of up to 25 per cent will be increased from 50 per cent to 100 per cent from 6 April 1996 (11). This allows all qualifying shareholdings to be passed on free of tax.

5.12 The inheritance tax relief for landlords of agricultural land introduced in the 1995 Finance Act will be amended to ensure consistent treatment of landlords in different parts of the country (*).

Employee share schemes

5.13 A number of changes will be made to improve the attractiveness of employee share schemes:

– the minimum amount which may be saved each month under approved savings-related share options schemes will be reduced from £10 to £5, and a three year savings contract will be added to the existing five and seven year contracts. Over a million people participate in these schemes. In future such schemes will be able to operate in conjunction with statutory employee share ownership trusts;

– the period during which shares appropriated to employees under approved profit sharing schemes must be held in trust to qualify for tax relief will be reduced from five to three years. Nearly a million people are taking part in these schemes; and

– a new tax relief for Company Share Option Plans will be introduced to enable companies to grant share options worth up to £20,000 to their employees. There will be no income tax to pay when the options are granted or exercised. Companies will not be able to grant options at a discount (12).

Other changes

5.14 Certain insurance benefits paid in the event of sickness or redundancy, such as mortgage protection, permanent health and a range of long-term care insurance, will be exempt from tax. The exemption will apply from 6 April 1996, but with retrospective effect for some benefits (13).

5.15 The maximum level of earnings for which pension provision may be made with tax relief (the "earnings cap") will be increased in line with statutory indexation to £82,200 (–).

5.16 Tax relief for vocational training for trainees aged 30 or over will be extended to full-time courses of between four weeks and a year from 6 May 1996 (14).

5.17   The annual limit on charitable donations qualifying for income tax relief under payroll giving schemes will be increased from £900 to £1,200, from 6 April 1996 (*).

5.18   Personal tax reliefs and tax credits which are currently available to citizens of Commonwealth countries and the Irish Republic will be extended to citizens of all countries within the European Economic Area, from 6 April 1996 (15).

5.19   The scales for assessing the benefit of free fuel provided by employers for private use in company cars will be increased by 5 per cent, in line with fuel prices, from 6 April 1996 (16). The scales are also used for employers' national insurance contributions (57) and VAT (29).

Business taxation

Direct tax   **5.20**   The small companies' rate of corporation tax will be reduced from 25 per cent to 24 per cent from 1 April 1996, cutting the marginal rate of tax on profits for some 350,000 companies (17). All three million unincorporated businesses which pay tax will benefit from the cuts in income tax.

5.21   The foreign income dividend scheme, introduced in 1993 to help companies with a substantial proportion of foreign profits, will be improved. The rules for international headquarters companies owned by foreign quoted companies will be made more flexible and changes will be made to the way foreign profits are calculated. The amendments will generally take effect from 28 November 1995 (18).

5.22   Tax relief will be given on equalisation reserves for certain non-life insurance business, for accounting periods ending on or after 23 December 1996. This change is linked to a new supervisory requirement for insurance companies to maintain equalisation reserves where claims are particularly volatile (19).

5.23   Tax rules for approved investment trusts will be modified to allow them to invest in rented housing, as announced in the Housing White Paper in June 1995. These housing investment trusts will be exempt from capital gains tax and pay the small companies' rate of corporation tax on their rental income (*). The aim is to increase the supply of private rented housing by increasing investment in this sector.

5.24   The stamp duty and stamp duty reserve tax rules will be adapted to cater for electronic share transfers under Crest, from 1 July 1996 (*).

National insurance **5.25**   The introduction of the landfill tax (see para. 5.55) will allow a cut in the main rate of employers' national insurance contributions of 0·2 per cent from April 1997 (53). This will reduce wage bills for employers by some £500 million and cut the marginal cost of employment.

5.26   In the 1994 Budget it was announced that employers who hire someone who has been out of work for two years or more will be able to get a full rebate of employer NICs for that person for up to one year, starting in April 1996. This rebate will be extended to cover people who have been on training schemes or in temporary work during the two year qualifying period of unemployment (55).

Business rates **5.27**   This Budget improves the transitional protection for businesses whose rates bills are increasing in real terms following the 1995 rates revaluation. The 1994 Budget introduced a scheme to limit the real increases in bills to 10 per cent for large properties, 7½ per cent for small properties and 5 per cent for small mixed domestic/non-domestic properties (such as shops with flats above). For 1996–97 these maximum real increases will be reduced to 7½ per cent, 5 per cent and 2½ per cent respectively. This change will be financed by an increase in the Exchequer contribution to the scheme (52). The remainder of the scheme's cost will continue to be met by limits on real rates reductions which remain unchanged.

5.28   The rate poundage for 1996–97 will be increased in line with the RPI for the year to September 1995.

Simplification and deregulation

Direct tax **5.29**   The rate of Class 4 national insurance contributions, paid by the self-employed, will be reduced from 7·3 per cent to 6 per cent (54), and the 50 per cent tax relief for these contributions will be withdrawn, from 6 April 1996 (20). These changes will simplify self-assessment tax returns for the self-employed and, taken together, will be broadly neutral in their impact.

5.30   The taxation of debt issued by corporate borrowers and all debt held by corporate investors will be simplified with effect from 1 April 1996. Borrowers will get tax relief for interest costs and issue discounts; and all returns to corporate investors on gilts, bonds and other debt will be taxed or relieved as income. Taxation of individual investors remains broadly unchanged (21).

5.31   Legislation on the financing of UK government debt will be amended to enable gilts to be "stripped" into their component coupon and principal payments, and associated changes will be made to their taxation. This will allow the development of a strips market in UK gilts (22).

5.32   UK banks and stockbrokers will no longer be required to deduct tax from foreign dividends and interest except where they exercise a custodian function on behalf of a UK investor, from Royal Assent (23).

5.33   Subject to certain conditions, lump sum compensation paid for mis-sold personal pensions or buyout contracts will be exempt from income tax and capital gains tax (*).

5.34   To assist the introduction of self-assessment, this Budget includes further measures to:

- align time limits for claims, elections and notices with the time limits for filing returns and amending self-assessments (*);

- clarify the rules for claiming some tax reliefs (–); and

- help employers calculate the value of cheap or interest-free loans provided to employees (*).

5.35   The current pay and file regime for corporation tax will be aligned more closely with self-assessment (*).

5.36   The Inland Revenue will undertake preparatory work on proposals to rewrite law relating to Inland Revenue taxes to make it clearer and simpler. This would reduce costs to businesses and help taxpayers meet their obligations under self-assessment.

5.37   Other simplification and deregulation measures are:

- a new statutory framework will be introduced for agreements between employers and the Inland Revenue under which employers may make a single payment to meet the tax due on minor benefits and expenses (*);

- payments of Jobfinder's Grant from 6 April 1995 will be exempt from tax (*);

- the tax treatment of payments made under short-term government pilot schemes will in future be set by secondary rather than primary legislation (–);

- tax payable when a company controlled by its directors, or a small group of people, makes a loan to one of the people who control it, will be payable nine months after the end of the accounting period in which the loan is made, instead of fourteen days. The change will apply to loans made in accounting periods ending on or after 31 March 1996 (*);

- where employers have not entered the fixed profit car scheme, employees who use their own car for business travel will be able to use the scheme's tax free mileage rates to calculate any tax due (*);

- the meaning of "bank" for tax purposes will be aligned with that for regulatory purposes (–);

- fees earned by pension funds through lending out investments will be exempt from tax (*);

–   the definition for tax purposes of shares on the Official List of the Stock Exchange will be amended in line with changes in the Stock Exchange (–); and

–   the tax treatment of certain financial transactions in overseas securities will be amended (*).

VAT   **5.38**   A number of changes are also proposed to simplify and deregulate VAT:

–   the annual turnover threshold above which traders must register for VAT will rise from £46,000 to £47,000 from 29 November 1995. The deregistration threshold will also rise by £1,000 to £45,000. The registration and deregistration thresholds for acquisitions from other Member States will increase from £46,000 to £47,000 on 1 January 1996 (28);

–   the payments on account scheme for large VAT payers is to be reformed from 1 June 1996, following consultation. The monthly payments on account will be halved and traders will be given the option of paying their actual monthly VAT liability instead. This will give businesses in the scheme a continuing cash flow benefit of some £35 million a year. Payment by electronic means will become mandatory, and the concession which allows electronic payments to be deferred for seven days will be withdrawn. Late payments will in future be subject to default surcharge (27);

–   the second VAT simplification directive will be implemented in UK law. The main provision is to introduce fiscal warehousing creating a VAT-free regime for trading in certain commodities (30);

–   the limit above which VAT has to be charged on business gifts will be raised from £10 to £15 from 29 November 1995 (*);

–   the special rules governing the VAT treatment of trading stamps will be abolished with effect from 1 June 1996 (*); and

–   Customs will be given discretion to allow traders to omit certain information from VAT invoices from the summer of 1996 (–).

Intrastat   **5.39**   From 1 January 1996, the annual threshold above which traders must provide Customs and Excise with detailed statistics on trade within the European Union will increase from £150,000 to £160,000 (–).

Anti-avoidance and revenue protection measures

Direct tax   **5.40**   Measures will be introduced to:

–   end a scheme for avoiding the full tax liability on the benefit of job-related living accommodation (24);

–   ensure that UK residents with an interest in non-resident companies are taxed appropriately on capital gains made by those companies (25);

- modify the existing provisions relating to controlled foreign companies (CFCs) to require trading CFCs to distribute at least 90 per cent of their taxable profits (less capital gains and foreign taxes) for accounting periods beginning on or after 28 November 1995 (26);

- require sub-contractors in the construction industry who are paid under deduction arrangements to have registration cards. Contractors will need to see the card before making any payment to the sub-contractor. This new requirement will not be introduced before 1 August 1998 (*); and

- amend the definition of companies exempt from certain anti-avoidance provisions to refer to those whose shares or stocks are on the Official List of the Stock Exchange (–).

VAT   **5.41**   To reduce the scope for avoidance or evasion of VAT, measures will be introduced to:

- counter VAT avoidance involving the transfer of companies or assets into or out of group registrations, with effect from 29 November 1995 (–);

- require businesses to issue a credit note or a debit note when a change in price alters the amount of VAT due after an invoice has been issued. Customs are consulting about the change which is expected to apply from the summer of 1996 (31);

- extend the special VAT accounting scheme for gold to cover all gold grain irrespective of purity or price, with effect from 29 November 1995 (32);

- provide for instances where the penalty for large errors in VAT returns is imposed to count towards the tally for the penalty for repeated errors, from Royal Assent (*); and

- restore the penalty for failure to notify liability to register for VAT when a business has been transferred as a going concern, with effect from 1 January 1996 (33).

Excise duties   **5.42**   Customs and Excise will be given powers to prevent fuel taxed for off road use in another Member State being used as road fuel for private vehicles in the UK. This is in line with existing powers for fuel in commercial vehicles. The measure will take effect from Royal Assent (*).

Excise duties

Alcohol **5.43**   Duties on beer, table wine, sparkling wine and most cider will remain unchanged (34). Duty on spirits will be reduced by 4 per cent from 6 pm on 28 November 1995 (35). From 1 January 1996, to give effect to a previous international agreement, duty on fortified wine will be reduced by 6·7 per cent (36). From 1 October 1996 a banded duty structure will be introduced for cider with the duty on very strong cider (over 7·5 per cent alcohol by volume) increased by 50 per cent from the current rate (37).

Tobacco **5.44**   Duties on most tobacco products will be increased from 6 pm on 28 November 1995, in line with the Government's commitment to increase duty on average by at least 3 per cent a year in real terms. Duty on hand-rolling tobacco will remain unchanged (38).

Oils **5.45**   The tax (duty plus VAT) on petrol and diesel will rise by 3·5 pence per litre, in line with the Government's commitment to increase duty on road fuels on average by at least 5 per cent a year in real terms (39). Duty on gas oil and fuel oil will also be raised by 5 per cent in real terms (41). The tax on road fuel gases (compressed natural gas and liquid petroleum gas) will be reduced by 5·8 pence per kg because these fuels produce markedly lower emissions of major pollutants (*). All these changes will take place at 6 pm on 28 November 1995. The tax on superunleaded petrol will be increased by a further 3·9 pence per litre from 15 May 1996, to remove a tax advantage which is not justified by the environmental effects of this product (40).

5.46 The changes in duty and their effect on the price of each product are set out below. Price effects include VAT except for gas oil and fuel oil.

Excise duty changes

	Change in duty (per cent)	Effect on price of typical item (pence)	Unit
Alcohol			
Beer	0	0	
Wine	0	0	
Sparkling wine	0	0	
Fortified wine	−6·7	−12	75cl bottle
Most cider and perry	0	0	
Very strong cider and perry	50	8	pint
Spirits	−4	−27	70cl bottle
Tobacco			
Cigarettes	7·5[1]	15	packet of 20
Cigars	6·9	6	packet of 5
Hand-rolling tobacco	0	0	
Pipe tobacco	6·9	8	25 grams
Fuel			
Leaded petrol	8·2	3·5	litre
Unleaded petrol	9·5	3·5	litre
Superunleaded petrol[2]	20·1	7·4	litre
Diesel	9·5	3·5	litre
Gas oil	8·9	0·2	litre
Fuel oil	8·9	0·1	litre
Road fuel gases	−15·0	−5·8	kg

[1] *Specific duty up 8·5 per cent. Rate of ad valorem duty unchanged.*
[2] *Increases in two stages. See paragraph 5.45.*

Betting   **5.47** Pool betting duty will be reduced by 5 per cent to 27½ per cent from 3 December 1995. It will be cut by a further 1 per cent to 26½ per cent from 5 May 1996, on condition that this is passed on to the Football Trust and the Foundation for Sport and the Arts (42). General betting duty will be reduced by 1 per cent to 6¾ per cent from 1 March 1996, subject to satisfactory agreement on how the cut will be spread between the betting industry and the horse and greyhound racing industries (43). These changes are a response to growing competition from the National Lottery.

5.48 Pools companies will be able to make returns and payments of pool betting duty monthly, rather than weekly as at present, from 31 December 1995 (42).

5.49 The rates of amusement machine licence duty are unchanged (44). The current practice of allowing machine-specific rather than premises-specific licences for most types of amusement machines will be given statutory cover from Royal Assent (–).

Air passenger duty **5.50**   The rates of air passenger duty are unchanged at £5 for flights to destinations in the European Economic Area and £10 elsewhere (45).

Vehicle excise duty **5.51**   Duty on private/light goods vehicles (PLG), chiefly cars, taxis and vans, will rise by £5 to £140 from 29 November 1995, in line with inflation (47). Duty on lorries will be frozen, the sixth successive Budget freeze for most rates of lorry VED (48).

5.52   An off road notification scheme will be introduced for all cars, taxis, vans, tricycles and motorcycles. Keepers of vehicles will be required to notify the Driver and Vehicle Licensing Agency (DVLA) when a vehicle excise licence is not to be renewed because the vehicle is taken off the road, sold, or scrapped. This will enhance DVLA's enforcement effort, reduce duty evasion, and improve the vehicle record (49).

5.53   Vehicles which are at least 25 years old in the PLG, tricycle and motorcycle classes will be exempt from VED from 29 November 1995 (50). Steam driven vehicles will be placed in the special concessionary class, paying annual duty of £35 (*).

5.54   A number of minor changes will be made to:

 —   enhance the ability to set automatic penalties (51);

 —   correct certain minor anomalies arising from the 1995 Finance Act (*); and

 —   move those heavy goods vehicles which have remained within the PLG class into the more appropriate special vehicles class (*).

Landfill tax

5.55   As announced in the 1994 Budget, a new tax on waste disposed of in landfill sites will be introduced on 1 October 1996. The tax is designed to use market forces to reduce the environmental damage associated with waste disposal. The tax will be based on weight and have two rates: £2 per tonne for inactive waste, which does not decay or contaminate land, and £7 per tonne for all other waste. Landfill operators will be able to claim a tax rebate of 90 per cent on payments to environmental trusts set up for specific purposes, up to a maximum of 20 per cent of their landfill tax bill (46).

National insurance contributions

5.56   From April 1996, the lower earnings limit will be increased from £58 to £61 a week, in line with the single person's rate of retirement pension; the earnings thresholds for the employers' lower rate bands will each be increased by £5 to £110, £155 and £210; and the upper earnings limit will be increased from £440 to £455 a week (56). The new structure of contributions is:

Structure of national insurance contributions from April 1996

Weekly earnings	Annual earnings[2]	Percentage NIC rate[1]	
		Employees	Employers[3]
Below £61	Below £3 172	0	0·0
£61 to £109·99	£3 172 to £5 720	2% of £61	3·0
£110 to £154·99	£5 720 to £8 060	plus 10%	5·0
£155 to £209·99	£8 060 to £10 920	of earnings	7·0
£210 to £455	£10 920 to £23 660	between £61	10·2[4]
Above £455	Above £23 660	and £455	10·2[4]

[1] *Not contracted out rates.*
[2] *Approximate annual equivalent.*
[3] *Rates apply to all earnings.*
[4] *To be reduced to 10·0 per cent from April 1997, subject to the usual statutory review by the Secretary of State for Social Security.*

5.57   The weekly Class 2 rate for the self-employed will be increased to £6·05 and the Class 3 voluntary contribution to £5·95. The lower and upper profits limits for Class 4 contributions will increase to £6,860 and £23,660 respectively (56).

5.58   Treasury grant not exceeding 6 per cent of contributory benefit expenditure will be made available to the National Insurance Fund in 1996–97. The Government Actuary will report on the likely effect of the changes on the Fund.

Table 5.1   Revenue effects of Budget measures

| | £ million   yield (+)/cost (−) of measure | | | |
| | Changes from a non-indexed base | Changes from an indexed base | | |
	1996–97	1996–97	1997–98	1998–99
INLAND REVENUE				
Personal taxation				
1 Personal allowance – up by £240	−1 070	−440	−640	−610
2 Age related personal allowances – up by £280/£290	−120	−40	−60	−70
3 Married couple's allowances – indexed	−90	0	0	0
4 Income limit for age related allowances – indexed	−10	0	0	0
5 Lower rate band – up by £700	−520	−370	−530	−510
6 Basic rate limit – up by £1,200	−270	−40	−80	−80
7 Basic rate – reduced to 24 per cent	−1 600	−1 600	−2 000	−2 100
Savings				
8 Tax on savings income cut to 20 per cent	−800	−800	−400	−450
Capital				
9 CGT retirement relief – age limit reduced	−10	−10	−40	−60
10 Inheritance tax threshold – increased to £200,000	−155	−130	−250	−295
11 IHT business relief extended	★	★	★	−5
Other personal tax measures				
12 Employee share schemes – changes	−15	−15	−10	−10
13 Insurance benefits exempted	−10	−10	−10	−10
14 Vocational training relief extended	★	★	−5	−10
15 Personal reliefs etc extended to EEA nationals	−10	−10	−20	20
16 Car fuel scales increased	10	10	10	10
Business taxation				
17 Small companies' corporation tax rate cut to 24 per cent	★	★	−95	−130
18 Foreign income dividend scheme – changed	−10	−10	−10	−10
19 Insurance equalisation reserves – tax relief	0	0	−100	−100
Simplification and deregulation				
20 Relief for Class 4 NICs – withdrawn	0	0	240	190
21 Taxation of gilts and bonds	★	★	★	★
22 Gilt strips market	0	0	★	★
23 Paying and collecting agents – simplified	−5	−5	★	★
Anti-avoidance measures				
24 Accommodation provided by employers	10	10	10	10
25 Capital gains of non-resident companies	5	5	20	30
26 Controlled foreign companies	0	0	0	★
CUSTOMS AND EXCISE				
Value added tax				
27 Payments on account – changes	600	600	0	0
28 Registration and deregistration thresholds increased	−10	10	10	5
29 Car fuel scales increased	5	5	10	10
30 Second VAT simplification directive	−25	−25	0	0
31 Credit notes	5	5	5	5
32 Extension of special accounting scheme for gold	5	5	5	5
33 Belated notification penalty	5	5	5	5

Table 5.1   Revenue effects of Budget measures—*continued*

	£ million yield (+)/cost (−) of measure			
	Changes from a non-indexed base	Changes from an indexed base		
	1996–97	1996–97	1997–98	1998–99
Excise duties on:				
34 beer, wine and most cider unchanged	0	−150	−150	−155
35 spirits cut by 4 per cent	−30	−60	−60	−65
36 fortified wine cut by 6·7 per cent	★	−5	−5	−5
37 very strong cider up by 50 per cent	5	5	10	15
38 tobacco up by 3 per cent real but hand-rolling unchanged[1]	25	25	25	30
39 petrol and diesel up by 3·5p a litre[1]	45	45	55	70
40 superunleaded petrol increased by further 3·9p a litre	25	25	25	25
41 fuel oil and gas oil up by 5 per cent in real terms	20	10	10	15
42 pools betting cut by 6 per cent	−35	−35	−35	−35
43 general betting cut by 1 per cent	−65	−65	−70	−70
44 amusement machine licences unchanged	0	−5	−5	−5
Other measures				
45 Air passenger duty – unchanged	0	−10	−15	−15
46 Landfill tax introduced at £2/£7 per tonne	110	110	450	460
VEHICLE EXCISE DUTY				
47 Car VED increased from £135 to £140	115	−5	−5	−5
48 Lorry VED unchanged	0	−20	−20	−20
49 Off road notification scheme	0	0	15	25
50 25 year old vehicles exempted	−15	−15	−15	−15
51 Other minor measures	0	0	0	5
BUSINESS RATES				
52 Business rates – transitional scheme amended	−135	−135	−95	−55
NATIONAL INSURANCE CONTRIBUTIONS				
53 Employer NICs – main rate reduced by 0·2 per cent	0	0	−495	−580
54 Class 4 NICs – rate reduced to 6 per cent	0	0	−270	−205
55 Employer NICs – rebate for long-term unemployed extended	−5	−5	−10	−10
56 Earnings thresholds increased	−120	0	0	0
57 Car fuel scales increased	0	0	5	5
TOTAL	**−4 145**	**−3 140**	**−4 590**	**−4 790**

★ = *Negligible.*

[1] *Tax increases previously announced and confirmed in this Budget*

5 per cent real increase in road fuel duties	*1 430*	*805*	*855*	*900*
3 per cent real increase in tobacco duties	*480*	*210*	*215*	*220*
Total	*1 910*	*1 015*	*1 070*	*1 120*

Annex A to Chapter 5
Explaining the costings

This annex explains how the effects of Budget measures on tax yield are calculated.

The general approach   **5A.1**   The revenue effect of a Budget measure is the difference between the tax yield from applying the pre-Budget and post-Budget tax regimes to the levels of total income and spending at factor cost expected after the Budget. The estimates do not therefore include any effect the tax changes themselves may have on overall levels of income and spending. They do however take account of other effects on behaviour where they are likely to have a significant effect on the yield, and any consequential changes in receipts from related taxes. For example, the estimated yield from increasing the excise duty on tobacco includes the change in the yield of VAT on that duty, and the change in the yield of VAT and other excise duties resulting from the new pattern of spending. Where the effect of one tax change is affected by the implementation of others the measures are costed in the order in which they appear in Table 5.1.

5A.2   In the non-indexed base column the pre-Budget regime is the regime of allowances, thresholds and rates of duty which applied before this Budget (including any measures, such as the real increase in fuel duties, previously announced but not yet implemented). The indexed base columns strip out the effects of inflation by assuming, in defining the pre-Budget regime, that allowances, thresholds and rates of duty are increased in line with prices in this and in future Budgets (again taking account of measures previously announced but not yet implemented). Measures announced in this Budget are assumed to be indexed in the same way in future Budgets.

5A.3   In calculating the indexed base we assume that each year excise duties rise in November (January for alcohol), and allowances and thresholds rise in April, in line with the assumed increase in the RPI over 12 months to the previous September. The commitments for real increases in fuel and tobacco duties are also built in. The assumptions are 2¼ per cent, 2 per cent and 2 per cent for September 1996, 1997 and 1998 respectively.

Notes on individual Budget measures

The numbers below refer to lines in Table 5.1.

Inland Revenue taxes   The cost of the following measures in a full year, against an indexed base, is:

      1   £590 million

      2   £60 million

      5   £490 million

      6   £70 million

      7   £1,800 million

      8   £400 million.

3, 4   The increases in allowances and limits are rounded according to statutory rules after being increased in line with the rise in the all items Retail Prices Index in the year to September 1995.

12   The new scheme is not expected to have any costs in the first three years. The cost in a full year is £80 million. The cost of the other changes in a full year is £30 million.

21   These measures are assumed to be broadly revenue neutral; the actual cost or yield will depend on future market movements.

22   The revenue effects of this measure depend on decisions on the stocks which can be stripped and the timing of the start of the strips market. There will be no effect on tax receipts in 1996–97.

24, 25   The yield represents the estimated direct effect of the measures with the existing level of activity. Without these measures there could be a more significant loss of revenue in the future.

26   The likely yield in a full year from this measure with the existing level of activity is £100 million. Without this measure there could be a more significant loss of revenue in the future.

Customs and Excise taxes

30   Implementation of the second VAT simplification directive affects the timing of payments, causing a one-off loss in 1996–97.

35   The non-indexed figure shows the loss from the 4 per cent duty cut on spirits while the indexed figure also includes the cost of not revalorising the duty.

42   The move from weekly to monthly payment has revenue effects only in 1995–96.

46   The revenue figure for landfill tax in 1996–97 is a part year figure because the tax is being introduced on 1 October 1996.

Revenue effects in 1995–96

A number of Budget measures have revenue effects in 1995–96. These are summarised below:

	Measures in 1995 Budget which have revenue effects in current year	£ million yield (+)/cost (−) of measure
		Changes from an indexed base
		1995–96
8	Tax on savings income cut	−50
30	Second VAT simplification directive	15
34–37	Alcohol	−40
38	Tobacco	5
39–41	Road fuel	10
42	Pool betting duty[1]	−15
48, 50	Vehicle excise duty	−10
Total		**−85**

[1] *Includes the move from weekly to monthly payment of pools duty.*

109

Annex B to Chapter 5
Tax changes announced before the Budget

This annex sets out a number of tax changes which were announced before the Budget, the effects of which are taken into account in the forecasts. Measures announced by the Chancellor on 8 December 1994, following the Government's decision not to proceed with the second stage increase in VAT on domestic fuel and power, were reflected in revised tables for the FSBR 1995–96 published by the Treasury in January 1995.

Table 5B.1   Measures announced since the 1994 Budget

| | £ million   yield (+)/cost (−) of measure | | | |
| | Changes from a non-indexed base | Changes from an indexed base | | |
	1996–97	1996–97	1997–98	1998–99
Inland Revenue taxes				
1 Gilt repo market	★	★	★	★
2 Deduction at source for certain rents	−30	−30	★	★
3 Debt held by associates of banks	−10	−10	★	★
4 Executive share option scheme	0	0	0	0
Customs and Excise taxes				
5 Annual VAT returns for small businesses	−65	−65	0	0
6 VAT exemption for dispensing spectacles	−45	−45	−45	−45
7 VAT group registration	50	50	50	50
8 Pool betting duty reduced	−30	−30	−30	−30
9 Amusement machine licence duty	−15	−15	−15	−15
Vehicle excise duty				
10 Changes to vehicle excise duty	−5	−5	−5	−5
Business rates				
11 Relief for village shops	−15	−15	−15	−15
Total	**−165**	**−165**	**−60**	**−60**

★ = *Negligible.*

Inland Revenue taxes   **5B.1**   Measures to improve the liquidity of the gilt market will take effect from 2 January 1996. These include payments of gilt interest gross in certain circumstances, the ending of tax rules which impeded financial transactions in gilts and new arrangements to collect tax on gilt interest from UK companies. The measures are estimated to have a cost of £100 million in 1995–96.

5B.2   The requirement to deduct tax at source from certain rents payable by mineral extraction, transport and similar businesses, was abolished for payments made on or after 1 May 1995.

5B.3 A measure in the 1994 Budget brought the tax liability of issuers of securities through dedicated subsidiaries of a bank into line with that which applies where banks lend money direct. A transitional provision was announced on 20 February 1995 to defer the application of this measure, where the issuer is a university or housing association, until 1 April 1996.

5B.4 The income tax relief available for share options granted under approved executive share option schemes will be withdrawn in relation to options granted on or after 17 July 1995. The yield in a full year is estimated to be £80 million.

Customs and Excise taxes **5B.5** On 22 September 1995 Customs and Excise announced an enhancement of the annual accounting arrangements for small traders with an annual turnover of less than £100,000.

5B.6 In March 1995 the High Court ruled that dispensing services associated with the supply of spectacles should be treated as a separate supply and should be exempt from VAT.

5B.7 New measures were announced to counter VAT avoidance involving the transfer of companies in or out of group registrations. The measures took effect from midnight on 28 February 1995.

5B.8 Pool betting duty was reduced by 5 per cent from 37·5 per cent to 32·5 per cent from 7 May 1995.

5B.9 Major changes involving types of machine, rates and the administration of the new amusement machine licence duty were announced on 31 March and 7 September 1995. All the changes took effect from 1 November 1995.

Vehicle excise duty **5B.10** A number of changes to VED were announced during the passage of the 1995 Finance Bill to exempt short journey agricultural vehicles; place all-terrain vehicles in the special concessionary class; create concessionary classes for recovery vehicles; and place small island HGVs in the special vehicles class.

Business rates **5B.11** The Government announced in the Rural White Paper proposals to introduce a new scheme of rate relief for village shops, at the discretion of local authorities.

Table 5B.2   Measures announced in 1994 Budget or earlier which take effect after 1995 Budget

| | £ million yield (+)/cost (−) of measure | | | |
| | Changes from a non-indexed base | Changes from an indexed base | | |
	1996–97	1996–97	1997–98	1998–99
Inland Revenue taxes				
12 Self-assessment	★	★	50	850
13 Construction industry tax scheme	0	0	0	400
Customs and Excise taxes				
14 5 per cent real increase in road fuel duties	1 695	1 070	2 120	3 335
15 3 per cent real increase in tobacco duties	545	275	525	795
16 Tour operators' margin scheme	10	10	10	10
Total	**2 250**	**1 355**	**2 705**	**5 390**

★ = *Negligible.*

Inland Revenue taxes   **5B.12**   As announced in the March 1993 Budget, the assessment and collection of personal tax is being reformed from 1996–97 with the introduction of self-assessment. The main measures:

– abolish the preceding year basis of assessment for the self-employed, and tax income as it arises from 1997–98, with a transitional year in 1996–97;

– align payment dates for assessed income tax from all sources and for capital gains tax;

– introduce separate assessment for partners; and

– introduce clear rules for filing tax returns and paying tax, and clear sanctions for failing to comply with them.

The November 1994 Budget announced further measures including simplification of the way income from property and income of non-residents are taxed; and a requirement for employers to give their employees certain information which they need to complete their tax returns. The figures in the table include Class 4 NICs.

5B.13   Changes to the construction industry tax scheme were introduced in the 1995 Finance Act which will ensure that only those businesses running more substantial construction operations will qualify for certificates exempting them from deductions for tax and national insurance contributions. The changes will not take effect before 1 August 1998.

Customs and Excise taxes   **5B.14**   The Chancellor said in the November 1993 Budget that road fuel duties would be increased on average by at least 5 per cent in real terms in future Budgets. The yield shown here and in line 15 of Table 5B.2 includes the effect of duty increases in future Budgets. The footnote to Table 5.1 shows only the yield from implementing the commitment in this Budget.

5B.15   The Chancellor said in the November 1993 Budget that tobacco duties would be increased on average by at least 3 per cent in real terms in future Budgets.

5B.16   On 25 October 1994 it was announced that the tour operators' margin scheme would be amended with effect from 1 January 1996 so that the standard rate of VAT would be applied to the whole of a tour operator's margin on holidays and travel within the Community. On 24 October 1995, following consultations with the trade, proposals were announced which would allow tour operators to alleviate the effects of the change.

6 Public spending

Introduction

6.01 The Government's objective is to reduce public spending as a share of national income over time and, within the total, to improve the use of resources and the efficiency of markets throughout the economy. Objectives for specific programmes will be set out in Departmental Reports published in March.

6.02 The plans for public spending set out in this Budget, which cover the three financial years from 1996–97 to 1998–99, will reduce public spending as a share of GDP by 3¼ percentage points and meet by 1997–98 the Government's objective of bringing spending to below 40 per cent as a share of national income.

The Control Total

6.03 The public spending objective is expressed in terms of the combined spending of central and local government – GGE(X). This is explained in the box on page 117. The Government seeks to achieve its objective by planning and controlling a narrower aggregate – the Control Total. The Control Total covers 85 per cent of total government spending. It differs from GGE(X) in that it excludes cyclical social security and debt interest, the two areas most affected by the economic cycle. There are a number of other differences giving rise to the accounting adjustments which are explained in Annex A.

1995–96 **6.04** The Control Total for 1995–96 is forecast to be £255·5 billion, slightly below the plans in the last Budget (after taking account of classification changes). Social security spending is forecast to be higher than planned, but this is more than covered by the unallocated Reserve of £3 billion within the Control Total.

New plans: summary **6.05**   Planned spending has been increased on priority programmes, including schools, the National Health Service and the police. These increases are funded from savings elsewhere. The costs of government are contained by tight control of departmental running costs, which are expected to fall by 12 per cent in real terms over the next three years. With greater private sector involvement in the provision of public services, through private finance and challenge funding, there is less need for direct investment by the Government. Indeed, the Government could not afford to maintain capital spending at existing levels while taking on long-term commitments to buy services from the private sector. Savings are also expected from a clampdown on social security fraud, and revenues will be protected by enhanced efforts to ensure compliance of taxpayers and prevent evasion of vehicle excise duty.

6.06   The Government aims to improve value for money from public expenditure and improve the supply-side performance of the economy. Expenditure measures to achieve this include reform of social security to improve work incentives, higher spending on schools, including special measures targeted at basic skills, more choice and variety in education and more apprenticeships and training for young people. The Government is also introducing more pilot schemes to help people back to work. There are additional resources for science and a number of programmes important for competitiveness and small businesses. These measures are reinforced by well-targeted infrastructure investment. In addition, firm control of the overall level of public spending has enabled the Government to improve incentives by reducing tax rates. These improvements are in the context of deregulated, open and competitive markets in which successful firms can flourish and the consumer gets better value for money.

The Control Total **6.07**   The Control Total for the next three years is set out in Table 6.1.

Table 6.1   The Control Total

	£ billion			
	1995–96	1996–97	1997–98	1998–99
Plans in 1994 Budget after classification changes	256·3	263·4	271·7	279.9
Control Total set out in this report	255·5	260·2	268·2	275·6
Reductions	−0·8	−3·2	−3·5	−4·3

6.08   The Control Total is planned to grow by 1¾ per cent in 1996–97, 3 per cent in 1997–98 and 2¾ per cent in 1998–99. On current projections of the GDP deflator, the real level of the Control Total is expected to increase by ¼ per cent in 1995–96, fall by 1 per cent in 1996–97 and grow by ½ per cent in each of the subsequent two years. Over the next three years taken together, the Control Total is expected to be broadly unchanged in real terms.

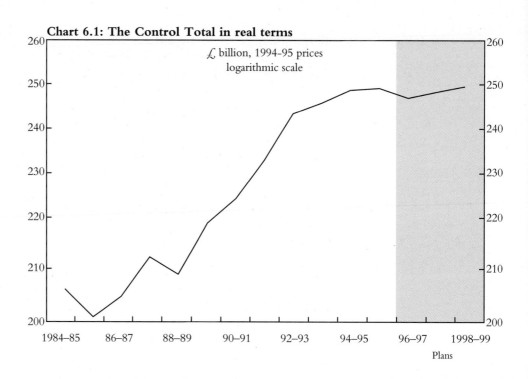

Chart 6.1: The Control Total in real terms

£ billion, 1994–95 prices
logarithmic scale

6.09 For the fourth year in succession, the Government's cash spending plans have been reduced below those set out in the previous year. This has partly been the result of lower than expected inflation, but the plans have also been reduced in real terms, as shown in Chart 6.2. Spending next year, 1996–97, will be £12 billion less than was projected when plans were first set in the 1993 Public Expenditure Survey.

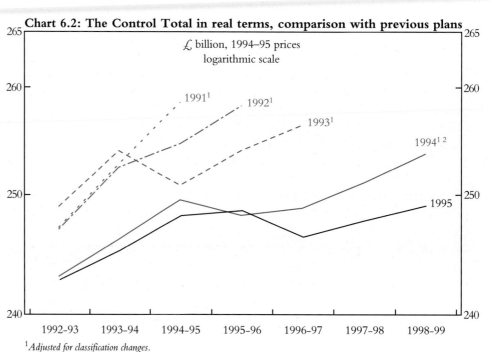

Chart 6.2: The Control Total in real terms, comparison with previous plans

£ billion, 1994–95 prices
logarithmic scale

[1] Adjusted for classification changes.
[2] Projection for 1998–99.

Other expenditure measures   **6.10**   In addition to measures which affect the Control Total, some measures in the Budget directly affect spending outside the Control Total. In particular, the Government has announced measures to reduce cyclical social security, as described in paragraph 6.74. Taking account of these, the overall Budget changes to planned public expenditure are set out in Table 6.2.

Table 6.2   Total Budget changes in public expenditure

	£ billion		
	1996–97	1997–98	1998–99
Cash terms			
Control Total	−3·2	−3·5	−4·3
Cyclical social security measures[1]	−0·1	−0·2	−0·2
Total Budget changes	**−3·3**	**−3·7**	**−4·5**

[1] See paragraph 6.74.

General government expenditure

6.11   The Government uses GGE(X) to measure its progress towards its objective of reducing public spending as a share of national income. This measure is based on national accounts aggregates.

The Government's expenditure target

In June 1995, the Chancellor announced that he was making two technical adjustments to the definition of the Government's public expenditure objective. The first was to exclude expenditure financed out of the proceeds of the National Lottery. The second was to treat debt interest on a net rather than a gross basis. The Chancellor explained that he was amending the objectives to ensure that when spending from Lottery proceeds increased this did not result in either the Government appearing to be less successful in meeting its objective or require further restraints on public expenditure.

This means that the Government's objective to reduce public expenditure as a share of national income over time is expressed in terms of general government expenditure, which is the combined expenditure of central and local government, with three adjustments. As in previous years GGE is adjusted to exclude privatisation proceeds (ie the objective is set gross of these receipts), expenditure out of the proceeds of the National Lottery is excluded, and receipts of interest and dividends from public corporations and the private sector are netted off. The resulting measure is referred to as GGE(X).

6.12   GGE(X) is projected to grow by 2¾ per cent a year on average over the next three years. On current projections of the GDP deflator, the real level of GGE(X) is expected to grow by ¾ per cent in 1995–96, fall by ½ per cent in 1996–97 and to grow by ½ per cent in 1997–98 and 1998–99. Over the next 3 years taken together, GGE(X) is expected to grow by less than ½ per cent in real terms. This is well below the projected growth rate of the economy, which means that GGE(X) is set to decline as a share of national income.

6.13   A detailed analysis of GGE(X) is set out in Table 6.3 below. Chart 6.3 shows the ratio of GGE(X) to GDP, which is expected to fall from 43½ per cent in 1992–93 to 38¾ per cent in 1998–99.

Table 6.3   The Control Total, GGE(X) and GGE[1]

	£ million							
	Outturn	Estimated outturn	New plans/projections			Changes from previous plans/projections		
	1994–95	1995–96	1996–97	1997–98	1998–99	1995–96	1996–97	1997–98
Central government expenditure[2]	174 464	181 100	184 000	188 000	191 900	1 000	−200	100
Local authority expenditure[3]	73 015	74 400	74 500	75 000	76 500	1 000	300	−400
Financing requirements of nationalised industries	750	−70	−840	120	−310	140	−180	400
Reserve			2 500	5 000	7 500	−3 000	−3 200	−3 700
Control Total	**248 229**	**255 500**	**260 200**	**268 200**	**275 600**	**800**	**3 200**	**−3 500**
Cyclical social security	14 351	14 000	13 900	14 200	14 700	−100	−100	−300
CG net debt interest	17 617	20 500	22 300	24 000	24 000	0	600	2 100
Accounting adjustments	9 023	9 600	9 700	9 100	9 600	800	−800	−1 800
GGE(X)	**289 220**	**299 600**	**306 100**	**315 500**	**324 000**	**−100**	**−3 500**	**−3 500**
Privatisation proceeds	−6 433	−3 000	−4 000	−2 500	−1 500	0	−1 000	−500
Other adjustments[4]	4 985	5 500	6 200	6 500	6 300	400	400	700
GGE	**287 772**	**302 100**	**308 300**	**319 500**	**328 700**	**300**	**−4 000**	**−3 300**
GGE(X) as a percent of GDP	42¾	42	40½	39¾	38¾	¼	−½	−¼

[1] *For definitions, rounding and other conventions, see notes in Annex A.*
[2] *Excluding cyclical social security.*
[3] *Comprises total central government support for local authorities and local authorities self-financed expenditure.*
[4] *Lottery-financed spending and interest and dividend receipts.*

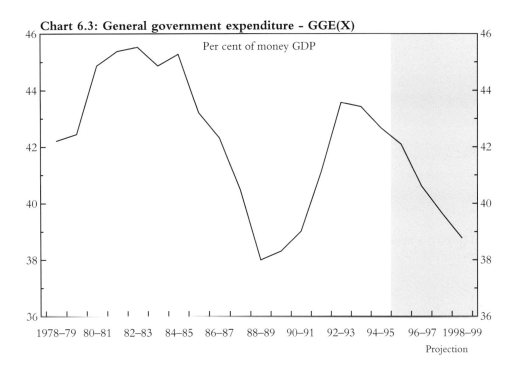

Chart 6.3: General government expenditure - GGE(X)

Per cent of money GDP

Projection

**Fundamental
expenditure reviews**

6.14   The changes in plans have been informed by the programme of fundamental expenditure reviews announced in February 1993 which has continued this year, with reviews of all remaining major departments, including Agriculture, Heritage, the Foreign and Commonwealth Office, Overseas Development Administration, the then Office of Public Service and Science and spending on the environment and the countryside. The reviews consider long-term trends in spending, and examine ways of delivering public services more economically and effectively. The programme of reviews will be completed by the end of this Parliament.

Capital spending

6.15   Table 6.4 shows total capital spending sponsored by the public sector. Over the Survey years, this is forecast to remain at or above £22 billion a year in cash terms; in real terms it is projected to remain above its level during most of the 1980s. It can be divided into direct public sector capital spending and spending under the Private Finance Initiative (PFI).

6.16   Capital spending directly financed by the public sector is expected to drop back from very high levels.

Table 6.4   Public sector capital expenditure[1]

	£ billion								
	Outturn					Estimated outturn	Projections		
	1990–91	1991–92	1992–93	1993–94	1994–95	1995–96	1996–97	1997–98	1998–99
Central government	9·6	10·3	10·9	10·1	9·1	8·5	8·1	7·8	7·6
Local authorities	5·9	7·0	7·2	6·7	7·1	7·5	6·5	6·2	5·9
Public corporations[2]	2·1	2·0	3·6	4·0	4·8	5·7	5·6	5·4	5·0
Notional allocation of the Reserve							0·3	0·5	0·8
Total public sector capital expenditure	**17·6**	**19·3**	**21·7**	**20·8**	**20·9**	**21·7**	**20·5**	**19·8**	**19·2**
Estimated capital expenditure under the Private Finance Initiative				0·3	0·3	0·6	1·9	2·6	2·8
Total publicly sponsored capital expenditure	**17·6**	**19·3**	**21·7**	**21·1**	**21·2**	**22·3**	**22·4**	**22·4**	**22·0**
Memo: Public sector capital[3]									
gross of depreciation	*20·7*	*21·6*	*23·5*	*21·6*	*21·3*	*22·5*	*20·5*	*19·9*	*19·3*
net of depreciation	*9·7*	*11·7*	*14·0*	*12·0*	*11·2*	*12·3*	*10·1*	*9·3*	*8·6*

[1] *Figures are shown for the national accounts definition of capital spending (including expenditure out of the proceeds of the National Lottery). See paragraph 6A.10.*
[2] *Excluding the capital expenditure of industries privatised or planned to be privatised before 31 March 1999.*
[3] *Including industries now privatised while they were in the public sector.*

6.17   This change in the balance between directly financed expenditure and privately financed investment is the result of the Government's reforms of the way in which public services are delivered. The programme of contracting out through the *Competing for Quality* initiative, and privately financed capital spending under the Private Finance Initiative, have turned the public sector in many areas into a purchaser rather than a provider of capital intensive services. Private sector management can often provide better services at lower cost to the taxpayer.

6.18   Challenge funding, by allocating public provision competitively, encourages partnership between the public and private sectors, gearing private money and expertise into public services. In many cases projects benefit from the involvement and commitment of local communities, helping to ensure that spending is well targeted.

6.19   In this and other ways the public sector is increasingly working through partnerships with the private sector. So, by themselves, the figures for conventional public capital spending figures can give a misleading picture of the level of investment in public services. When the government buys services from the private sector, investment undertaken by the companies that provide the services is not counted as public sector investment; it is, however, deployed to meet public needs.

Public and private partnership: private finance

6.20   The Private Finance Initiative was launched in 1992, and the Private Finance Panel was established the following year. Resources for the Panel, now chaired by Sir Christopher Bland, are being substantially increased this year.

6.21   Under the Private Finance Initiative, the public sector does not contract to buy assets: it contracts to buy services. The private sector decides how best to provide those services, with investment as one of the inputs. Because their own money is at risk, the private sector has an incentive to supply services cost-effectively. PFI deals that have already been completed show substantial value for money benefits compared with conventional procurement.

6.22   By the end of 1998–99, Departments expect to have agreed PFI contracts involving capital expenditure worth some £14 billion. This figure could well be exceeded: the Private Finance Panel have identified over 1,000 potential projects worth £25 billion for the Government to consider. Capital expenditure under PFI commitments is expected to run at about £2 billion or more a year over the next three years (see Table 6.5 which presents an illustrative profile based on agreed and likely PFI projects). Total expenditure on the services purchased under these contracts will be much greater still.

Table 6.5   Private Finance Initiative: estimated capital spending

	1996–97	1997–98	1998–99	Total
	£ million			
Defence	30	80	210	320
FCO/ODA	10	10	10	30
Agriculture	10	20	10	40
Trade and Industry[1]	10	10	10	30
Education and Employment[2]	20	40	50	110
Transport	1 120	1 320	1 260	3 700
Environment[3][4]	30	30	30	100
Home Office	50	110	60	220
Legal departments	10	20	10	40
National Heritage	20	30	30	80
Health	170	200	300	670
Social Security[1]	130	70	100	300
Scotland[5]	140	360	420	920
Wales	60	150	150	360
Northern Ireland	50	80	80	210
Chancellor's departments	40	40	30	110
Total	**1 900**	**2 570**	**2 760**	**7 240**

[1] Joint Benefits Agency/Post Office Counter project recorded against Social Security.
[2] Excludes private finance activity in education institutions classified to the private sector. See paragraph 6.45.
[3] Docklands Light Railway.
[4] In addition about £4–5 billion a year of private investment is levered in through housing, urban regeneration and other programmes.
[5] Includes Forestry Commission.

6.23   The Chancellor announced last year that contracts worth £5 billion would be agreed in the course of this year. That target is well on the way to being met. It includes a number of major infrastructure projects. Competition is underway for one of Europe's largest construction projects, the Channel Tunnel Rail Link. The contracts for the first four design, build, finance and operate (DBFO) road projects are expected to be awarded in the next few weeks, with another four in Spring 1996. The Department of Transport will shortly be launching five more DBFO road projects, worth £500 million. In total, over £1 billion a year of capital spending on transport PFI projects is expected over each of the next three years – a significant addition to national investment in transport.

6.24   It is not only transport that is benefiting from private finance. Projects worth about £250 million are likely to be approved in the Health Service by the end of 1995–96, many of them for redevelopment and improvement of services in district general hospitals. One such scheme, which has been approved, is the £35 million modernisation of the High Wycombe and Amersham sites of the South Buckinghamshire NHS Trust. Other examples of PFI projects include the redevelopment of government offices, water and sewerage facilities, prisons, and provision of information technology for government and other public services. Local authorities and public corporations as well as central government are benefiting. The projects range across the whole of the United Kingdom, providing a huge and varied opportunity for business in the construction, manufacturing and service industries.

6.25   A further set of PFI-related changes to the English and Welsh local government capital finance regulations was announced on 31 October and will be implemented from April 1996. These measures will give authorities greater freedom to harness private investment in the replacement and upgrading of buildings through, for example, DBFO arrangements. The Local Authority Associations have decided to set up their own Private Finance Unit, to start operations at the beginning of 1996–97.

Public and private partnership: challenge funding

6.26   The challenge funding approach to public spending complements the opportunities for bringing private sector resources and expertise into the delivery of public services that are available through the PFI.

6.27   Challenge principles have already been successfully used by some departments, most notably in urban regeneration projects. The first bidding round for new regeneration projects supported by the Single Regeneration Budget was held in 1994. Two hundred bids were successful and are now receiving funding for projects. The successful bids drew together a wide range of partners from the public, private and voluntary sectors. The second round winners will be announced shortly and there will be further bidding rounds in 1996 and 1997.

6.28   All departments are now exploring the options for extending the principles into new areas across the full range of government activities. New plans include challenge funds for transfer of deprived housing estates to private landlords, schools renewal and tackling housing benefit fraud.

Public sector pay and Civil Service running costs

Public sector pay   **6.29**   The Government's approach to public sector pay, as reaffirmed by the Chancellor in his statement on 18 September, is that pay increases should be offset, or more than offset, by efficiencies and other economies. The cost of pay settlements will need to be contained within expenditure provision.

Running costs   **6.30**   Provision for the running costs of civil departments, which was £15·1 billion in 1995–96, has been set at £14·8 billion in 1996–97, £14·6 billion in 1997–98 and £14·3 billion in 1998–99. Compared with previous plans, provision has been reduced by £270 million in 1996–97 and £380 million in 1997–98.

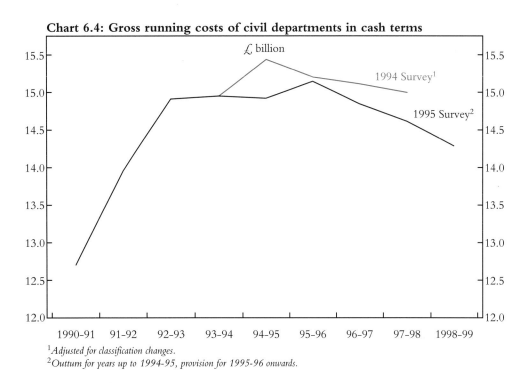

Chart 6.4: Gross running costs of civil departments in cash terms

[1]Adjusted for classification changes.
[2]Outturn for years up to 1994-95, provision for 1995-96 onwards.

6.31   Chart 6.4 shows that having been held broadly flat since 1992–93, running costs will be reduced in cash terms in each of the next three years, and plans for 1998–99 are more than 5 per cent lower than for 1995–96. By 1998–99, the annual cost of the Civil Service will be £1·9 billion – over 12 per cent – lower in real terms than in 1995–96, as shown in Chart 6.5.

Chart 6.5: Gross running costs of civil departments in real terms

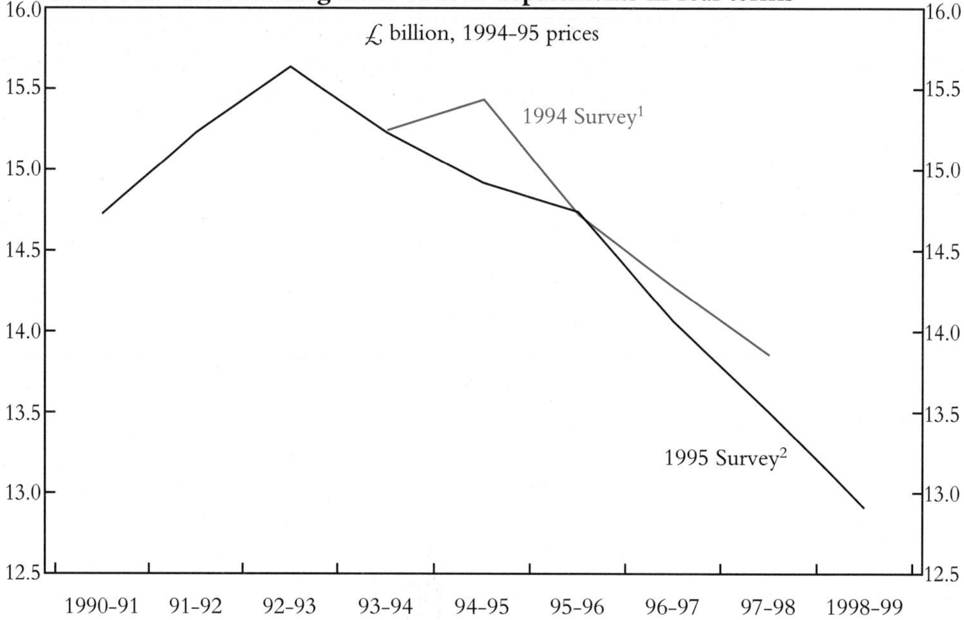

£ billion, 1994-95 prices
16.0
15.5
15.0
14.5
14.0
13.5
13.0
12.5
1994 Survey1
1995 Survey2
1990-91
91-92
92-93
93-94
94-95
95-96
96-97
97-98
1998-99

[1] *Adjusted for classification changes.*
[2] *Outturn for years up to 1994-95, provision for 1995-96 onwards.*

6.32 Running costs plans have been reduced for almost all departments, but they take account of government priorities and pressures, including a growing prison population, the introduction of the Jobseeker's Allowance and the need to protect the PSBR by safeguarding revenue collection and benefit payments, and to implement anti-fraud measures. Chart 6.6 shows how the plans for 1996–97 are split between the major departments.

Chart 6.6: Gross running costs of civil departments in 1996–97

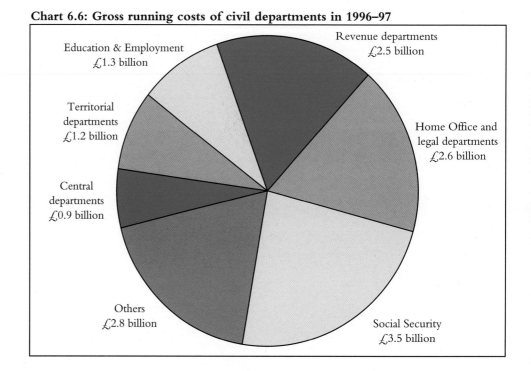

Revenue departments £2.5 billion
Home Office and legal departments £2.6 billion
Social Security £3.5 billion
Others £2.8 billion
Central departments £0.9 billion
Territorial departments £1.2 billion
Education & Employment £1.3 billion

End year flexibility for running costs

6.33   End year flexibility for running costs has recently been extended to improve the use of resources and avoid surges in spending at the end of the year. The scheme allows departments to manage their running costs budgets sensibly from year to year by carrying forward underspends to add to provision in a later year.

6.34   As a result of constraints on their running costs budgets, departments have underspent in anticipation of greater pressures in future years. In 1994–95, they spent £510 million less than provision, as shown on Chart 6.4, and the underspend available for carry forward is now £360 million.

MOD operating costs

6.35   Ministry of Defence administration costs are subsumed within a wider operating costs control, covering all defence costs except for the procurement of major equipment and related research. MOD operating costs are planned to fall in cash terms in 1995–96 and in each of the next three years. The new plans are £16·5 billion in 1996–97, falling to £16·2 billion in 1998–99.

The new plans

6.36   Table 6.6 analyses the Control Total by department showing changes from previous plans. Central government support for local authorities and the financing requirements of nationalised industries have been attributed to the appropriate departments.

Table 6.6   Control Total by department[1]

	£ million							
	Outturn	Estimated outturn	New plans			Changes from previous plans		
	1994–95	1995–96	1996–97	1997–98	1998–99	1995–96	1996–97	1997–98
Defence	22 562	21 210	21 420	21 910	22 620	−500	−500	−400
Foreign Office	1 264	1 470	1 090	1 110	1 110	310	−70	−70
Overseas Development	2 369	2 370	2 290	2 370	2 420	10	−130	−110
Agriculture, Fisheries and Food	2 430	2 930	3 020	2 960	2 920	−100	10	0
Trade and Industry – Programmes	2 806	3 240	3 200	3 130	3 120	30	50	−50
Trade and Industry – Nat Inds	579	430	−290	−190	−270	−60	−40	480
ECGD	−11	30	10	0	−10	40	0	0
Transport	5 937	4 620	4 180	4 660	4 410	240	−190	−350
DOE – Housing	7 173	6 700	5 840	5 660	6 050	−10	−880	−1 100
DOE – Urban and environment	2 475	2 370	2 400	2 270	2 050	40	70	−40
DOE – Local government[2]	29 913	30 320	31 320	31 380	31 530	10	430	530
Home Office	6 258	6 600	6 520	6 640	6 760	170	50	−10
Legal departments	2 596	2 710	2 720	2 750	2 890	−90	−170	−140
Education and Employment[3]	13 573	14 190	14 040	14 510	14 520	−10	−430	120
National Heritage	984	1 020	960	940	940	20	0	10
Health	31 502	32 930	33 750	34 180	34 970	0	520	120
of which NHS	*30 578*	*31 980*	*33 050*	*33 910*	*34 700*	*0*	*120*	*130*
Long term care[4]			60	60	60		60	60
Social Security[5]	70 405	73 730	76 810	79 600	82 250	1 160	1 040	550
Scotland	14 078	14 470	14 550	14 690	14 800	30	−70	10
Wales	6 557	6 720	6 800	6 830	6 860	−60	−70	−100
Northern Ireland[5]	7 408	7 820	8 010	8 210	8 270	110	130	190
Chancellor's departments	3 351	3 300	3 200	3 120	3 100	30	−60	−100
Cabinet Office	944	1 120	960	970	930	170	100	80
European Communities	1 235	2 890	2 300	2 500	2 500	70	−470	−140
Local authority self-financed expenditure	11 761	12 300	12 500	13 000	13 300	600	600	700
Reserve			2 500	5 000	7 500	−3 000	−3 200	−3 700
Control Total	**248 229**	**255 500**	**260 200**	**268 200**	**275 600**	**−800**	**−3 200**	**−3 500**

[1] For definitions, rounding and other conventions, see notes in Annex A. See Annex B for the composition of each departmental grouping.

[2] Includes payments of Revenue Support Grant and National Non-domestic Rates to English local authorities. These finance, at local authorities' discretion, a range of local services, including education, social services and other environmental services.

[3] Does not include local authority Total Standard Spending on education.

[4] The long term care package is described in paragraph 1.11. Attribution to departments has not yet been finalised.

[5] Excluding cyclical social security.

Departmental detail

Defence   **6.37**   The new plans for defence spending are consistent with the Government's commitment to maintain stability in front line forces while increasing efficiency and cutting out waste. The forecast pattern of expenditure on equipment means that the defence budget is expected to be significantly underspent in 1995–96. These savings will be carried forward into 1996–97 and 1997–98. In addition, the Ministry of Defence intends to transfer ownership of the married quarters estate in England and Wales to the private sector.

Foreign and Commonwealth Office   **6.38**   The new plans take account of the savings that are expected from greater efficiency, including from the fundamental expenditure review, and greater use of private finance for capital spending. The Foreign and Commonwealth Office will continue to give high priority to the inward investment and export promotion effort which has been considerably enhanced in recent years.

Overseas Development   **6.39**   The reduction in plans reflects significantly lower projections of the cost to the UK of multilateral aid. The proposed allocations will enable the UK to maintain a well-focused, substantial bilateral aid programme. The UK will remain the fifth largest donor in the world.

Agriculture, Fisheries and Food   **6.40**   The new plans for agriculture reflect an increase in the estimated cost of agricultural support under the Common Agricultural Policy. This is largely the result of a lower than expected "green pound", which determines the rate at which CAP support prices set in ecu are converted into national currency. These increases are largely balanced by savings on domestic spending.

Trade and Industry – programme spending   **6.41**   The cash plans for DTI programmes and spending on science have been increased next year compared to the plans in last year's Budget. This will permit further development of the competitiveness and small business programmes, including the development of Business Links and support for exports, innovation and good management.

Science and Technology   **6.42**   Total central government spending on science and technology in 1996–97 is expected to be about £6 billion, broadly the same as in 1995–96.

Trade and Industry – nationalised industries   **6.43**   Provision is made for an increase in Nuclear Electric's external financing limit (EFL) following the privatisation of the company's Advanced Gas cooled Reactor (AGR) and Pressurised Water Reactor (PWR) power stations in 1996, and for a reduction in the Post Office's EFL.

Education and Employment

6.44   Planned public spending on education in England next year will rise in real terms. This includes an increase for current spending on schools of £878 million – some 5 per cent in cash terms. Within this, £774 million will be channelled through the local authority settlement. Provision has been made to double the number of pupils entering the Assisted Places Scheme and to introduce nursery vouchers for all four year olds. Current spending on higher and further education remains as planned and will finance an increase of 50,000 students in further education, and continue to provide for around one in three young people to go into higher education. The new plans provide for continued expansion in the number of grant maintained schools.

6.45   The new plans for education and employment reflect the significant scope for private finance. This will build on the considerable private investment in education which already occurs. By September 1995 further education colleges and universities had raised about £1·6 billion from commercial sources. Private finance will make an increasing contribution to the capital needs of universities, colleges and grant maintained schools. Private funding could add £430 million in 1996–97, £390 million in 1997–98 and £355 million in 1998–99 over and above public funding for higher and further education and grant maintained schools. Within these totals commercial borrowing is expected to form a declining share as deals which involve a greater degree of risk transfer increase.

6.46   Long-term unemployment has fallen by 12 per cent over the past year. The Government has taken only part of that reduction into account in making a consequential reduction in planned spending on employment and training programmes. There is provision to double the number of Modern Apprenticeships and, with the ending of Community Action, for new ways of helping the long-term unemployed.

Transport

6.47   The new plans for transport reflect the priority given to public transport. Spending on national roads, and central government support for spending on local roads and transport, have been reduced compared to previous plans. Substantial investment in transport infrastructure will continue. There is over £4 billion a year of publicly financed spending, together with £1 billion a year of investment under the Private Finance Initiative. Tenders will soon be invited for five more design, build, finance and operate road projects, in addition to the eight projects which have already gone out to tender.

Transport – nationalised industries

6.48   The department's programmes include the financing of railways, together with the external financing limits of London Transport and the Civil Aviation Authority. Savings on railways reflect the scope for increased efficiency.

6.49   Investment in London Transport (including the Jubilee Line Extension) next year will remain at this year's record level of over £1 billion. This is supplemented by PFI investment, including in Northern Line trains.

DOE – Housing and Environment 6.50 Reduced spending on housing reflects the high level of output achieved in recent years, to which lower unit costs and greater use of private finance have contributed. The plans also include anticipated receipts from the sale of the Housing Corporation loan book. Housing Revenue Account Subsidy is set at a level that encourages efficiency savings from local authority housing management and maintenance. A new challenge fund has been established to facilitate the transfer of poor quality local authority stock to housing associations and other landlords.

6.51 The plans include £250 million for third and fourth bidding rounds for funds from the Single Regeneration Budget. The first round will lever in private investment of over £2½ billion.

Home Office 6.52 The Government continues to give high priority to the fight against crime. The new plans allow an additional 5,000 police officers over the next three years, and a challenge funding package to provide 10,000 more closed circuit TV (CCTV) cameras in town centres. About 4,000 additional prison places will be provided, and resources have been made available to implement security improvements and an enhanced anti-drug programme. Increased resources have also been provided to deal with asylum claims.

Legal departments 6.53 The new plans for the legal departments take account of lower forecasts of spending on legal aid, and allow for the introduction of standard fees for civil cases.

National Heritage 6.54 The cash plans for the Department of National Heritage are broadly unchanged. The department's programmes will benefit from resources released by efficiency savings.

National Lottery 6.55 The National Lottery is expected to provide around £1¼ billion a year for projects relating to the arts, sport, heritage, charities and the celebration of the new millennium. This is in addition to the Government's expenditure plans. Spending of Lottery money counts as general government expenditure, but is excluded from the Government's target for reducing spending as a share of national income measured by GGE(X), and is outside the Control Total.

Health 6.56 Provision for the Health Service continues to grow in real terms, more than meeting the Government's manifesto commitment. Spending on the NHS in England will increase by over £1 billion next year. In addition, patients will benefit from improvements in efficiency including NHS management savings, worth around £650 million next year. These will all be ploughed back into patient care, on top of the increase in overall resources.

6.57 By April 1995 the NHS had benefited from well over £100 million worth of private finance. Several large hospital private finance schemes are due to complete the procurement process and receive approval in 1995–96, with a total capital value of around £250 million. The first of these large projects – a £35 million scheme for modernisation of two of the South Buckinghamshire NHS Trust's hospital sites – has been approved, and by the end of next year it is expected that projects worth £1 billion will have come forward for approval. During 1996–97 it is expected that the private sector will invest around £165 million in NHS facilities and these figures are expected to be exceeded in subsequent years.

Long-term care package

6.58 As part of the package of measures to help meet the costs of long-term care, the levels of capital below which people become eligible for help for care in residential and nursing homes have been increased. These changes are described in paragraph 1.11 in Chapter 1. The Government has provided for reimbursement to local authorities and the Departments of Social Security to compensate for the extra spending which will result.

Social Security

6.59 The social security plans incorporate revised estimates of the number of claimants and provide for the uprating of benefits every year (subject to paragraph 6.60 below). The assumptions used for benefit upratings and for unemployment are set out in Annex A.

6.60 The new plans reflect the Government's intention to narrow the gap between lone parents' benefit rates and those paid to other families. In April 1996 one parent benefit and the lone parent premiums will not be uprated. Next year these benefits will be integrated into the main family benefit structure. The Secretary of State for Social Security will need to look at all the relevant factors each year before reaching conclusions on the appropriate benefit rates for lone parents and other families. However, for expenditure planning purposes, it is assumed that the restructured lone parent benefits will remain at the same cash level in future years.

6.61 The plans also reflect a reform of housing benefit for the under 25s which will restrict housing benefit to the cost of shared accommodation. This will give young people a real incentive to rent within their means and diminish any artificial incentive to leave home.

6.62 The plans also include measures to ensure that benefits do not go to economic migrants who claim asylum in order to get round the immigration rules; and enhanced measures to combat fraud, including increased home visits and, in particular, greater emphasis on tackling housing benefit fraud. By 1998–99 social security anti-fraud measures are expected to save about £2½ billion a year.

Scotland, Wales and Northern Ireland **6.63**   Changes in these programmes reflect in the main the effect of changes in comparable programmes in England. Each Secretary of State has wide discretion about the distribution of expenditure within his programme. Detailed plans will be announced shortly.

Chancellor's departments **6.64**   The expenditure of the Chancellor's departments is largely accounted for by the Inland Revenue and Customs and Excise. The costs of administering the Chancellor's departments continue to fall in cash terms, reflecting the continued drive for improved efficiency. Within falling overall resources, Customs' intelligence and investigation capability is being enhanced by over 200 posts, and compliance activity by the revenue departments is being protected.

European Community **6.65**   Compared with the previous forecast, net payments to European Community institutions are higher in 1995–96, but lower thereafter. The lower forecast for 1996–97 reflects a higher level of Structural Funds receipts and an anticipated underspend of the 1995 Community budget. The underspend is expected to generate a surplus which will be recovered in 1996, reducing member states' contributions to the budget in that year.

6.66   Net payments also fluctuate for a number of other reasons, including the timing of payment of UK contributions, adjustments made to UK contributions in earlier years, and subsequent correction of the UK abatement. The forecast reflects the latest UK and Community economic assumptions, changes to estimates of UK customs duties and the VAT base, and the UK abatement. The cumulative benefit of the abatement since 1984 is expected to be around £18 billion by the end of 1995–96. The value of the abatement in 1996–97 is forecast to be around £1·9 billion.

The Reserve **6.67**   The Reserve has been set at £2½ billion for 1996–97, a further £2½ billion in 1997–98 (making £5 billion in all), and a further £2½ billion in 1998–99 (£7½ billion in all). Calls on the Reserve will be reduced by the expected receipts from the transfer to the private sector of the Ministry of Defence married quarters estate, but will include departments' use of end year flexibility, and the continuation of the 80:20 central funding scheme for early departure costs announced in the 1994 Civil Service White Paper *Continuity and Change*.

6.68 The Reserve included in last year's plans for 1996–97 was £5¾ billion, reduced from £6 billion when a package of measures was announced on 8 December 1994 following the vote in the House of Commons on VAT on fuel and power. During the course of the Public Expenditure Survey, £3¼ billion has been used, as intended, to cover the costs of new policies and demands, like extra provision for schools, police and health, and to cover increased estimates of the costs of demand-led programmes such as social security. The remaining £2½ billion is left unallocated to meet new priorities and unavoidable increases that may emerge during the next year. The reduction in the Control Total has been achieved by identifying savings elsewhere in the spending plans.

The Reserve

The Control Total set in the Budget for each of the next three years is an upper limit on public spending. Most of the total is allocated to particular programmes. But the Government has to retain some margin for manoeuvre so that it can respond to unexpected events and pressures without breaching the overall limit. Therefore part of the Control Total, called the Reserve, is left unallocated. The Government is planning to spend all the Control Total including the Reserve but it has not yet decided exactly how.

The Reserve is always larger for the second and third years of the planning period than for the first. That is because there is more uncertainty about the further future and because, very often, a decision to increase spending on a programme in the first year will feed through automatically into extra spending in later years thus pre-empting part of the Reserves for those years.

The Government's spending plans in this Budget include Reserves of £2½ billion for 1996–97, £5 billion for 1997–98, and £7½ billion for 1998–99. In effect the Reserve in 1997–98 allows for £2½ billion commitments entered into in 1996–97 and a further £2½ billion to deal with events in 1997–98.

Local authorities

6.69 Local authorities are responsible for setting their own spending budgets. These are financed by support provided by central government and from local authorities' own resources. Table 6.7 summarises the projections of local authority spending, showing the new plans for central government support and projected local authority self-financed expenditure (LASFE). The Government intends to use its powers to cap local authority budgets, if that proves necessary.

6.70   In 1996–97, Total Standard Spending (TSS) in England – that is, the amount which central government thinks it is appropriate for local authorities to spend on revenue expenditure – has been set at £44·9 billion, including provision for the costs of local government reorganisation. Adjusting for transfers, the increase compared to 1995–96 is 3·3 per cent. This includes year on year increases of:

  – £774 million (4·5 per cent) for education;

  – £481 million (6·9 per cent) for personal social services, including care in the community; and

  – £235 million (4·0 per cent) for police services.

Table 6.7   Local authority expenditure[1]

				£ million				
	Outturn	Estimated outturn	New plans			Changes from previous plans		
	1994–95	1995–96	1996–97	1997–98	1998–99	1995–96	1996–97	1997–98
Current								
Aggregate External Finance[2]								
England	34 349	34 770	35 650	35 420	35 710	70	870	590
Scotland[3]	5 299	5 320	5 380	5 310	5 300	10	110	70
Wales[3]	2 416	2 460	2 510	2 480	2 520	0	70	50
Total Aggregate External Finance	**42 064**	**42 550**	**43 560**	**43 220**	**43 530**	**90**	**1 040**	**700**
Other current grants	13 746	14 090	13 510	14 040	15 990	350	−970	−1 390
Total current	**55 811**	**56 640**	**57 070**	**57 260**	**58 530**	**430**	**70**	**−700**
Capital								
Capital grants	1 472	1 900	1 760	1 630	1 510	60	−10	−80
Credit approvals	3 971	3 580	3 180	3 190	3 140	−70	−360	−270
Total capital	**5 443**	**5 480**	**4 940**	**4 820**	**4 650**	**−10**	**−370**	**−360**
Total central government support to local authorities	**61 254**	**62 100**	**62 000**	**62 100**	**63 200**	**400**	**−300**	**−1 100**
Local authority self-financed expenditure	**11 761**	**12 300**	**12 500**	**13 000**	**13 300**	**600**	**600**	**700**
Total local authority expenditure	**73 015**	**74 400**	**74 500**	**75 000**	**76 500**	**1 000**	**300**	**−400**

[1] For definitions, rounding and other conventions, see Annex A.

[2] Aggregate External Finance includes Revenue Support Grant, distribution of Non-domestic Rate revenue and a number of specific grants which fund part of the expenditure on a specific service or activity.

[3] Scottish and Welsh figures for 1997–98 and 1998–99 are illustrative; final figures will depend on the Secretary of State's decisions on the allocation of resources.

6.71   Other current grants outside Aggregate External Finance (AEF) are projected to fall by £1 billion in 1996–97 and £1·4 billion in 1997–98 compared with previous plans. The bulk of this reduction reflects lower housing benefit expenditure arising from reduced caseload growth, lower real rent increases and policy savings, including measures to combat fraud, set out in paragraphs 6.60 to 6.62.

6.72 Gross capital expenditure by local authorities has been inflated in recent years by the temporary relaxation of the capital receipts rules which was announced in the 1992 Autumn Statement. Gross capital spending is expected to be somewhat lower in 1996–97, at £8¼ billion. Capital receipts are projected to be around £3 billion, and net capital spending around £5 ¼ billion.

Other public expenditure

6.73 In addition to expenditure within the Control Total, GGE(X) also includes cyclical social security, privatisation proceeds, and net debt interest.

Cyclical social security   **6.74** Cyclical social security is defined as unemployment benefit (from 1996–97, the Jobseekers' Allowance) and income support paid to people of working age. Cyclical social security is forecast to fall in real terms reflecting the improved prospects for inflation and unemployment. There are also measures which are estimated to reduce planned cyclical social security spending by a further £100 million in 1996–97 and £200 million in each of the subsequent years. The majority of these savings come from proposals affecting asylum seekers and the anti-fraud measures set out in paragraphs 6.60 to 6.62.

Accounting adjustments   **6.75** The accounting adjustments are needed to reconcile the Control Total aggregate with the national accounts aggregates including GGE. They are explained in more detail in paragraph 6A.15. They are expected to be lower during the years covered by the new plans because of the effect of the sale of Nuclear Electric's AGR and PWR power stations.

Privatisation proceeds   **6.76** Privatisation proceeds are projected to be £4 billion in 1996–97, £2½ billion in 1997–98 and £1½ billion in 1998–99.

Debt interest   **6.77** General government net debt interest is projected to rise from £20½ billion in 1995–96 to £23¾ billion in 1998–99.

Table 6.8   Debt interest

	Outturn	Projections			
	1994–95	1995–96	1996–97	1997–98	1998–99
General government					
Gross	22·6	25·6	27·0	28·5	28·3
Receipts	5·0	5·2	4·8	4·7	4·5
Net	17·6	20·4	22·2	23·9	23·8
Central government					
Gross	22·1	25·1	26·5	28·0	27·9
Receipts	4·5	4·6	4·1	4·0	3·8
Net	17·6	20·5	22·3	24·0	24·0

£ billion

Annex A to Chapter 6
Public expenditure analyses

This annex includes a number of more detailed analyses of expenditure. It also explains the conventions used in presenting the figures throughout Chapter 6.

Rounding conventions 6A.1 For tables presenting the new plans the following conventions apply:

Future years: Departments' spending totals within the Control Total are rounded to the nearest £10 million (except for non-cyclical social security in 1997–98 and 1998–99, which is rounded to £50 million). The Control Total and spending sector totals (except financial requirements of the nationalised industries), items outside the Control Total, and projections of capital spending are rounded to the nearest £100 million.

1995–96: The figures for 1995–96 are department's best view of outturn. The rounding conventions adopted for future years also apply here to reflect their provisional nature.

6A.2 For tables which show the Control Total and GGE(X) in real terms, all figures are rounded to the nearest £100 million. Projections of capital spending in real terms are also rounded to the nearest £100 million.

6A.3 Changes and totals in the tables are based on unrounded figures. They may therefore differ from the changes and sums of the rounded figures.

6A.4 Some figures may be subject to detailed amendment before the publication of the Statistical Supplement early in 1996.

Assumptions for planning public expenditure 6A.5 The economic assumptions used in the public expenditure plans are set out below. The assumptions that underlay the 1994 Budget plans are also shown. The assumptions for the GDP deflator in 1995–96 and 1996–97 are consistent with the short-term forecast described in Chapter 3. Those for later years, and all other figures, are assumptions not forecasts.

Economic assumptions for public expenditure

		Percentage changes on a year earlier unless otherwise stated			
		1995–96	1996–97	1997–98	1998–99
GDP deflator	1995 Budget	2¾	2¾	2½	2¼
	1994 Budget	3¼	2½	2¼	
Retail prices index[1]	1995 Budget	3·9	2¼	2	
(September)	1994 Budget	3	2½		
Rossi index[1]	1995 Budget	3	2¼	2	
(September)	1994 Budget	2¼	2¼		
Average earnings	1995 Budget	3½	4		
	1994 Budget	4½			
GB unemployment	1995 Budget	2·18	2·1	2·1	2·1
(millions)	1994 Budget	2·4	2·4	2·4	
Northern Ireland	1995 Budget	87	87	87	87
unemployment	1994 Budget	95	95	95	
(thousands)					

[1] *Used for projecting social security expenditure in the following financial year.*

Calculation of changes previous plans and projections

6A.6   Changes from previous plans are differences from the plans and projections for 1995–96 to 1997–98 in the February 1995 Statistical Supplement after account is taken of classification changes and transfers and switches between departments.

6A.7   The most significant such items included in this Report are the transfer of responsibilities from the former Department of Employment to the Department for Education and Employment, the Department of Trade and Industry and others. Responsibility for Science has been transferred from the Cabinet Office to the Department of Trade and Industry.

6A.8   There is only one material classification change affecting the aggregate figures. In last year's Budget, BNFL was reclassified as a public corporation. The figures for the plans in last year's FSBR have been revised to reflect changes in the basis on which external finance is calculated. There are a few minor classification changes but none which affect the Control Total by more than £10 million in any year.

Real terms figures

6A.9   Figures in real terms are cash levels adjusted to 1994–95 price levels by excluding the effects of general inflation as measured by the GDP deflator.

Measurement of capital spending

6A.10   The main analysis set out in Table 6.4 shows the expenditure components of the public sector's capital account, on national accounting definitions but excluding industries which have been privatised or are planned to be privatised before 31 March 1999. These differ from the Control Total measure in a number of respects described in paragraph 6A.15, the main one being the treatment of VAT refunds. The figures include:

(i)   gross domestic fixed capital formation, ic expenditure on fixed assets – schools, hospitals, roads, computers, plant and machinery etc. This is measured net of receipts from sales of fixed assets (eg council houses and surplus land);

(ii)   grants in support of capital spending by the private sector;

(iii)   the value of the physical increase in stocks (for central government, primarily agricultural commodity stocks).

6A.11   Estimates of depreciation of the public sector's stock of fixed assets are based on the national accounts series produced by the Central Statistical Office (in Table 14.3 of the Blue Book), together with projections by the Treasury.

Central government expenditure

6A.12   This includes the financing requirements of trading funds and public corporations other than the nationalised industries. Cyclical social security spending is excluded from the measure of central government spending within the Control Total.

Local authority self-financed expenditure

6A.13   Local authority self-financed expenditure is the difference between total local authority expenditure, including gross debt interest but net of capital receipts, and central government support to local authorities (ie AEF, specific grants and credit approvals).

Central government net debt interest

6A.14   Central government debt interest is shown net of receipts of interest and dividends from outside general government.

Accounting adjustments   **6A.15**   The accounting adjustments include various items within GGE(X) but outside the Control Total (other than central government debt interest and cyclical social security, which are shown separately). The larger items are non-trading capital consumption, refunds of VAT, teachers' and NHS pensions increase payments, the difference between Civil Service and armed forces pensions payments and accruing superannuation liability charges, and the debt remuneration element of NHS Trusts' charges to health authorities. The net market and overseas borrowing of nationalised industries and other public corporations is, on the other hand, within the Control Total but outside GGE(X) such that net repayments add to the magnitude of the accounting adjustments. Debt interest paid from local authorities to central government reduces the accounting adjustments. This is removed to avoid double counting between local government debt interest payments (which are shown inside local authority expenditure) and central government debt interest. Local authority receipts of interest and dividends are netted off here. Fuller details of the national accounting adjustments are given in the Statistical Supplement.

Table 6A.1 Public expenditure, 1963–64 to 1998–99

	Control Total[1]		GGE(X)			Privatisation proceeds	General government expenditure	Money GDP[2]	Adjusted GDP deflator
	£ billion	Real terms[3] £ billion	£ billion	Real terms[3] £ billion	Per cent of GDP[2]	£ billion	£ billion	£ billion	Index (1994-95 =100)
1963–64			10·9	121·4	35½		11·3	31·4	9·0
1964–65			11·8	125·5	35		12·3	34·2	9·4
1965–66			13·1	132·9	36½		13·6	36·6	9·8
1966–67			14·5	141·0	38		15·1	38·9	10·3
1967–68			16·8	159·1	41½		17·5	41·2	10·6
1968–69			17·5	157.8	40		18·2	44·6	11·1
1969–70			18·5	158·6	39¼		19·3	48·0	11·7
1970–71			20·7	163·7	39½		21·6	53·2	12·6
1971–72			23·3	168.8	40		24·4	59·3	13·8
1972–73			26·4	177·0	39¾		27·6	67·6	14·9
1973–74			30·5	191·4	41½		32·0	75·0	15·9
1974–75			41·0	215·2	46¾		42·9	89·4	19·1
1975–76			51·6	215·8	47¼		53·8	111·2	23·9
1976–77			57·0	210·1	44¾		59·6	130·0	27·1
1977–78			61·7	199·9	41½	−0·5	63·9	151·3	30·8
1978–79			72·0	210·1	42¼		75·0	173·7	34·3
1979–80			87·0	217·3	42½	−0·4	90·0	208·6	40·0
1980–81			104·8	221·3	44¾	−0·2	108·6	237·7	47·3
1981–82			116·3	224·0	45½	−0·5	120·5	261·0	51·9
1982–83			127·8	229·8	45½	−0·5	132·7	285·8	55·6
1983–84			136·6	234·7	44¾	−1·1	140·4	310·0	58·2
1984–85	126·0	206·2	147·7	241·6	45¼	−2·0	150·8	332·1	61·1
1985–86	129·6	200·9	154·9	240·2	43¼	−2·7	158·5	364·9	64·5
1986–87	136·0	204·8	163·3	245·8	42¼	−4·5	164·6	392·7	66·4
1987–88	148·6	212·4	172·9	247·1	40½	−5·1	173·5	434·8	70·0
1988–89	156·1	209·1	180·7	242·1	38	−7·1	179·8	484·1	74·6
1989–90	175·1	219·3	198·0	248·0	38¼	−4·2	200·9	525·8	79·9
1990–91	193·5	224·4	217·3	251·9	39	−5·3	218·2	556·8	86·3
1991–92	213·2	232·6	238·6	260·4	41	−7·9	236·2	580·5	91·6
1992–93	231·6	242·8	263·6	276·4	43½	−8·2	260·6	605·2	95·4
1993–94	240·8	245·3	277·9	283·1	43½	−5·4	277·3	639·9	98·2
1994–95	248·2	248·2	289·2	289·2	42¾	−6·4	287·8	677·8	100·0
1995–96	255·5	248·7	299·6	291·6	42	−3·0	302·1	712	102·8
1996–97	260·2	246·4	306·1	289·9	40½	−4·0	308·3	754	105·6
1997–98	268·2	247·8	315·5	291·5	39¾	−2·5	319·5	795	108·2
1998–99	275·6	249·1	324·0	292·8	38¾	−1·5	328·7	836	110·6

[1] *Figures for the Control Total are only available on a consistent basis for the years shown. Figures are estimated outturn for 1995–96 and plans for 1996–97 onwards.*

[2] *An adjusted series for money GDP is used in the calculation of the ratio for years up to 1989–90. This has been constructed to remove the distortion caused by the abolition of domestic rates.*

[3] *Cash figures adjusted to price levels of 1994–95.*

Table 6A.2   GGE(X): plans and outturn[1]

	Per cent of GDP								
	1990–91	1991–92	1992–93	1993–94	1994–95	1995–96	1996–97	1997–98	1998–99
February 1991 Supplement (Cm 1520)	39	38¾	38¾	38½					
February 1992 Supplement (Cm 1920)	39	40¾	41¼	41	40½				
January 1993 Supplement (Cm 2219)	39¼	41¼	44	45	44¼	43¼			
February 1994 Supplement (Cm 2519)	39	41¼	43¾	44¼	43	42½	41¾		
February 1995 Supplement (Cm 2821)	39	41	43½	43½	43	41¾	41	40	
This Budget	39	41	43½	43½	42¾	42[2]	40½	39¾	38¾

Plans

Outturn

[1] Figures for GGE in previous publications have been adjusted for all subsequent classification changes, and general government interest and dividend receipts, which underlay those publications, have been subtracted.
[2] Estimated.

Table 6A.3 Control Total by department[1]

£ million

	Outturn					Estimated outturn	New plans			Changes from previous plans		
	1990–91	1991–92	1992–93	1993–94	1994–95	1995–96	1996–97	1997–98	1998–99	1995–96	1996–97	1997–98
Defence	21 709	22 913	22 910	22 757	22 562	21 210	21 420	21 910	22 620	-500	-500	-400
Foreign Office	968	1 132	1 278	1 276	1 264	1 470	1 090	1 110	1 110	310	-70	-70
Overseas Development	1 737	1 994	2 140	2 234	2 369	2 370	2 290	2 370	2 420	10	-130	-110
Agriculture, Fisheries and Food	2 137	2 159	2 198	2 938	2 430	2 930	3 020	2 960	2 920	-100	10	0
Trade and Industry – Programmes	2 707	2 714	2 809	2 735	2 806	3 240	3 200	3 130	3 120	30	50	-50
Trade and Industry – Nat Inds	1 903	1 702	1 300	1 278	579	430	-290	-190	-270	-60	-40	480
ECGD	372	215	117	-60	-11	30	10	0	-10	40	0	0
Transport	4 692	5 391	6 604	6 001	5 937	4 620	4 180	4 660	4 410	240	-190	-350
DOE – Housing	6 725	7 422	8 156	7 733	7 173	6 700	5 840	5 660	6 050	-10	-880	-1 100
DOE – Urban and environment	1 777	1 927	2 223	2 562	2 475	2 370	2 400	2 270	2 050	40	70	-40
DOE – Local government	20 522	28 356	31 175	29 378	29 913	30 320	31 320	31 380	31 530	10	430	530
Home Office	4 845	5 525	5 830	5 972	6 258	6 600	6 520	6 640	6 760	170	50	-10
Legal departments	1 640	2 001	2 334	2 415	2 596	2 710	2 720	2 750	2 890	-90	-170	-140
Education and Employment[2]	8 963	9 298	10 053	12 845	13 573	14 190	14 040	14 510	14 520	-10	-430	120
National Heritage	778	883	1 004	976	984	1 020	960	940	940	20	0	10
Health	22 461	25 544	28 213	29 773	31 582	32 930	33 750	34 180	34 970	0	520	120
of which NHS	*22 326*	*25 354*	*27 971*	*28 951*	*30 578*	*31 980*	*33 050*	*33 910*	*34 700*	*0*	*120*	*130*
Long term care[3]							60	60	60			60
Social Security[4]	48 932	55 219	61 839	67 862	70 405	73 730	76 810	79 600	82 250	1 160	1 040	550
Scotland	9 717	11 697	12 699	13 559	14 078	14 470	14 550	14 690	14 800	30	-70	10
Wales	4 441	5 309	5 992	6 305	6 557	6 720	6 800	6 830	6 860	-60	-70	-100
Northern Ireland[4]	5 525	6 018	6 580	7 085	7 408	7 820	8 010	8 210	8 270	110	130	190
Chancellor's departments	3 405	3 502	3 478	3 392	3 351	3 300	3 200	3 120	3 100	30	-60	-100
Cabinet Office	262	304	1 014	1 066	944	1 120	960	970	930	170	100	80
European Communities	2 027	707	1 898	1 873	1 235	2 890	2 300	2 500	2 500	70	-470	-140
Local authority self-financed expenditure	15 288	11 246	9 761	8 806	11 761	12 300	12 500	13 000	13 300	600	600	700
Reserve							2 500	5 000	7 500	-3 000	-3 200	-3 700
Control Total	**193 533**	**213 177**	**231 606**	**240 757**	**248 229**	**255 500**	**260 200**	**268 200**	**275 600**	**-800**	**-3 200**	**-3 500**

[1] For definitions, rounding and other conventions, see notes on page 136. See Annex B for the composition of each departmental grouping.
[2] Does not include local authority expenditure on education.
[3] The long term care package is described in paragraph 1.11. Attribution to Departments has not yet been finalised.
[4] Excluding cyclical social security.

Table 6A.4   Control Total by department in real terms[1]

| | | | | | | £ billion | | | |
| | Outturn | | | | | Estimated Outturn | | New plans | |
	1990–91	1991–92	1992–93	1993–94	1994–95	1995–96	1996–97	1997–98	1998–99
Defence	25·2	25·0	24·0	23·2	22·6	20·6	20·3	20·3	20·4
Foreign Office	1·1	1·2	1·3	1·3	1·3	1·4	1·0	1·0	1·0
Overseas Development	2·0	2·2	2·2	2·3	2·4	2·3	2·2	2·2	2·2
Agriculture, Fisheries and Food	2·5	2·4	2·3	3·0	2·4	2·9	2·9	2·7	2·6
Trade and Industry – Programmes	3·1	3·0	2·9	2·8	2·8	3·1	3·0	2·9	2·8
Trade and Industry – Nat Inds	2·2	1·9	1·4	1·3	0·6	0·4	-0·3	-0·2	-0·2
ECGD	0·4	0·2	0·1	-0·1	0·0	0·0	0·0	0·0	0·0
Transport	5·4	5·9	5·9	6·1	5·9	4·5	4·0	4·3	4·0
DOE – Housing	7·8	8·1	3·6	7·9	7·2	6·5	5·5	5·2	5·5
DOE – Urban and environment	2·1	2·1	2·3	2·6	2·5	2·3	2·3	2·1	1·9
DOE – Local government	23·8	30·9	32·7	29·9	29·9	29·5	29·7	29·0	28·5
Home Office	5·6	6·0	6·1	6·1	6·3	6·4	6·2	6·1	6·1
Legal departments	1·9	2·2	2·4	2·5	2·6	2·6	2·6	2·5	2·6
Education and Employment	10·4	10·1	10·5	13·1	13·6	13·8	13·3	13·4	13·1
National Heritage	0·9	1·0	1·1	1·0	1·0	1·0	0·9	0·9	0·8
Health	26·0	27·9	29·6	30·3	31·6	32·0	32·0	31·6	31·6
of which NHS	*25·9*	*27·7*	*29·3*	*29·5*	*30·6*	*31·1*	*31·3*	*31·3*	*31·4*
Long term care[2]							0·1	0·1	0·1
Social Security[3]	56·7	60·3	64·8	69·1	70·4	71·8	72·8	73·6	74·3
Scotland	11·3	12·8	13·3	13·8	14·1	14·1	13·8	13·6	13·4
Wales	5·1	5·8	6·3	6·4	6·6	6·5	6·4	6·3	6·2
Northern Ireland[3]	6·4	6·6	6·9	7·2	7·4	7·6	7·6	7·6	7·5
Chancellor's departments	3·9	3·8	3·6	3·5	3·4	3·2	3·0	2·9	2·8
Cabinet Office	0·3	0·3	1·1	1·1	0·9	1·1	0·9	0·9	0·8
European Communities	2·4	0·8	2·0	1·9	1·2	2·8	2·2	2·3	2·3
Local authority self-financed expenditure	17·7	12·3	10·2	9·0	11·8	12·0	11·9	12·0	12·0
Reserve							2·4	4·6	6·8
Control Total	**224·4**	**232·6**	**242·8**	**245·3**	**248·2**	**248·7**	**246·4**	**247·8**	**249·1**

[1] 1994–95 prices. For definitions, rounding and other conventions, see notes on page 136. See Annex B for the composition of each departmental grouping.
[2] The long term core package is described in paragraph 1.11. Attribution to Departments has not yet been finalised.
[3] Excluding cyclical social security.

Table 6A.5　Financing requirements of the nationalised industries, by department and industry[1]

£ million

	Outturn					Estimated outturn	New plans			Changes from previous plans		
	1990–91	1991–92	1992–93	1993–94	1994–95	1995–96	1996–97	1997–98	1998–99	1995–96	1996–97	1997–98
Trade and Industry	**1 903**	**1 702**	**1 300**	**1 278**	**579**	**430**	**−290**	**−190**	**−270**	**−60**	**−40**	**480**
British Coal[2]	890	605	791	1 400	742	60	100	50	0	0	50	30
British Shipbuilders	28	−9	−10	−9	11	0	−20	0	0	0	−20	0
Electricity (England and Wales)[3]	985	1 180	991	726	483	370	40	190	160	100	150	650
Post Office	0	−74	−80	−186	−235	−210	−300	−320	−310	0	−120	−140
British Nuclear Fuels			−392	−653	−422	210	−120	−120	−120	−160	−100	−50
Transport	**1 615**	**2 052**	**2 998**	**2 244**	**2 370**	**1 310**	**1 340**	**1 930**	**1 710**	**200**	**40**	**−90**
Railways[4]	1 077	1 464	2 064	1 461	1 541	340	430	1 290	1 290	140	−80	−120
Civil Aviation Authority	64	34	51	91	46	40	−10	−20	−20	10	−20	−20
London Transport	474	554	883	693	783	940	950	660	440	50	130	50
DOE – Environment	**48**	**50**	**48**	**49**	**48**	**50**	**50**	**50**	**50**	**0**	**0**	**0**
British Waterways Board	48	50	48	49	48	50	50	50	50	0	0	0
Scotland	**−114**	**−34**	**32**	**34**	**−27**	**−20**	**30**	**80**	**110**	**0**	**10**	**20**
Caledonian MacBrayne	5	9	13	12	11	10	10	10	10	0	0	
Electricity (Scotland)[5]	−108	−45	14	−28	−46	−40	20	60	90	0	10	30
Scottish Transport Group	−13	−2	0	44	0	0	0			0	0	
Highlands and Islands Airports[6]	2	4	5	6	8	10	10	10	0	0	0	0
Total[7]	**3 452**	**3 770**	**4 378**	**3 605**	**2 970**	**1 760**	**1 130**	**1 860**	**1 590**	**140**	**10**	**420**

[1] For definitions, rounding and other conventions, see notes on page 136.
[2] Future plans cover the cost of residual liabilities after privatisation.
[3] The Regional Electricity Companies, the National Grid Company, PowerGen and National Power were privatised during 1990–91. From 1991–92 comprises Nuclear Electric.
[4] Includes the financing requirements of British Rail, Railtrack, Union Railways, and European Passenger Services and other grants to the railway industry including those from the Office of Passenger Rail Franchising. (Some grants paid in Scotland are also included in the total in Scotland in Table 6.6).
[5] Scottish Power and Scottish Hydro-Electric were privatised during 1991–92. From 1992–93 comprises Scottish Nuclear.
[6] Highlands and Islands Airports Ltd, formerly part of the Civil Aviation Authority, became the responsibility of the Scottish Office from April 1995.
[7] This differs from the Nationalised Industries line of Table 6.3 because it includes railway grants mentioned above.

Annex B to Chapter 6
Departmental groupings

Short title used in tables	Departments covered
Defence	Ministry of Defence
Foreign Office	Foreign and Commonwealth Office – Diplomatic Wing
Overseas Development	Foreign and Commonwealth Office – Overseas Development Administration
Agriculture, Fisheries and Food	Ministry of Agriculture, Fisheries and Food The Intervention Board
Trade and Industry – Programmes	Department of Trade and Industry – Programmes Office of Fair Trading Office of Telecommunications Advisory, Conciliation and Arbitration Service Office of Electricity Regulation Office of Gas Supply
Trade and Industry – Nat Inds	British Coal British Shipbuilders Electricity (England and Wales) Post Office British Nuclear Fuels Limited
ECGD	Export Credits Guarantee Department
Transport	Department of Transport Office of the Rail Regulator Office of Passenger Rail Franchising
DOE – Housing	Department of Environment – Housing
DOE – Urban and environment	Department of Environment – Other Environmental Services Health and Safety Commission Office of Water Services Ordnance Survey Property Holdings PSA Services
DOE – Local government	Department of Environment – mainly block and transitional grants to English local authorities
Home Office	Home Office Charity Commission

Legal departments	Lord Chancellor's Department
	Crown Office, Scotland and Lord Advocate's Department
	Crown Prosecution Service
	Northern Ireland Court Service
	Public Record Office
	Serious Fraud Office
	Treasury Solicitor's Department
	Land Registry
Education and Employment	Department for Education and Employment
	Office for Standards in Education
National Heritage	Department of National Heritage
	Office of the National Lottery
Health	Department of Health
Social Security	Department of Social Security
Scotland	Scottish Office
	Electricity (Scotland)
	Forestry Commission
	General Register Office (Scotland)
	Scottish Courts Administration
	Scottish Record Office
	Registers of Scotland
Wales	Welsh Office
	Office of Her Majesty's Chief Inspector of Schools in Wales
Northern Ireland	Northern Ireland Office and Departments
Chancellor's departments	HM Treasury
	Office for National Statistics
	Crown Estate Office
	Department for National Savings
	Government Actuary's Department
	HM Customs and Excise
	Inland Revenue
	National Investment and Loans Office
	Registry of Friendly Societies
	Royal Mint
	Paymaster General's Office
Cabinet Office	Cabinet Office
	Office of Public Service
	Privy Council Office
	Central Office of Information
	Her Majesty's Stationery Office
	House of Commons
	House of Lords
	National Audit Office
	Parliamentary Commissioner and Health Service Commissioners
European Communities	Net payments to European Community institutions

List of abbreviations

ACT	Advance Corporation Tax
AEF	Aggregate External Finance
AGR	Advanced Gas-cooled reactor
Blue Book	UK national accounts
BNFL	British Nuclear Fuels Limited
CAA	Civil Aviation Authority
CAP	Common Agricultural Policy
CBI	Confederation of British Industry
CGBR	Central Government Borrowing Requirement
CGBR(O)	Central Government Own Account Borrowing Requirement
CGT	Capital gains tax
CTRL	Channel Tunnel Rail Link
DBFO	Design, Build, Finance and Operate
DCS	Defence Costs Study
DFEE	Department for Education and Employment
DOE	Department of the Environment
DSS	Department of Social Security
DTI	Department of Trade and Industry
DVLA	Driver and Vehicle Licensing Agency
ECGD	Export Credits Guarantee Department
ECU	European Currency Unit
EEA	European Economic Area
EFL	External Financing Limit
ERI	Effective exchange rate index
EU	European Union
FCO	Foreign and Commonwealth Office
FE	Further Education
FSBR	Financial Statement and Budget Report
FT-SE	Financial Times All Share index
G7	Major seven industrial countries
G10	Group of ten industrial countries comprising: Belgium, Canada, France, Germany, Italy, Japan, Netherlands, Sweden, Switzerland, UK and US
GDP	Gross Domestic Product
GGE	General Government Expenditure
GGE(X)	General Government Expenditure (see boxed text page 117 for detail)
GGR	General Government Receipts
GGBR	General Government Borrowing Requirement
GGBR(O)	General Government Own Account Borrowing Requirement
GGFD	General Government Financial Deficit

GM	Grant maintained
HGV	Heavy Goods Vehicle
IHT	Inheritance tax
IT	Information Technology
LABR	Local Authority Borrowing Requirement
LASFE	Local authority self-financed expenditure
LFS	Labour Force Survey
MIPs	Mortgage Interest Payments
MOD	Ministry of Defence
Money GDP	Gross Domestic Product in current market prices
MTFS	Medium-Term Financial Strategy
M0	Narrow measure of money stock
M4	Broad measure of money stock
NAIRU	Non-accelerating inflation rate of unemployment
NHS	National Health Service
NICs	National insurance contributions
ODA	Overseas Development Administration
OECD	Organisation for Economic Cooperation and Development
OPS	Office of Public Service
PCBR	Public Corporations Borrowing Requirement
PCMOB	Public Corporations' Market and Overseas Borrowing
PFI	Private Finance Initiative
PH	Property Holding
PLG	Private/Light Goods Vehicle
PSA	Property Services Agency
PSBR	Public Sector Borrowing Requirement
PSFD	Public Sector Financial Deficit
PWR	Pressurised Water Reactor
RPI	Retail Prices Index
SDR	Special Drawing Right
TSS	Total Standard Spending
VAT	Value added tax
VED	Vehicle excise duty

List of tables

List of charts

Data sources and definitions

A note detailing data sources and definitions covering Chapters 3 and 4 is available from HM Treasury. Copies are available free of charge to personal callers and for a postage and handling fee of £2.50 by post. Cheques should be made payable to HM Treasury and sent to Miss C T Coast-Smith, Public Enquiry Unit, Room 110/2, Treasury Chambers, Parliament Street, London SW1P 3AG. Telephone 0171-270 4458.

Printed in the United Kingdom for HMSO
Dd 5067079   11/95   C80   48003   Ord 338389